Adventurers and Pathfinders Living for Jesus

By

Dr Mandela Thyoka

Copyright © 2024 Dr Mandela Thyoka

ISBN: 978-1-917129-81-7

All rights reserved, including the right to reproduce this book, or portions thereof in any form. No part of this text may be reproduced, transmitted, downloaded, decompiled, reverse engineered, or stored, in any form or introduced into any information storage and retrieval system, in any form or by any means, whether electronic or mechanical without the express written permission of the author.

Cover photo courtesy of North American Division of Seventh-day Adventists. All other photos courtesy of the author.

Table of Contents

Preface

Introduction

Why Living for Jesus?

The Beginnings

How to start your own club

Adventurer Programme

Adventurer Awards

Pathfinder Programme

Pathfinder Honours

Club Curricula

Club Activities

Family

Church

School and Community

Teen Leadership Training

Master Guide

Adventurer and Pathfinder Bible Experience

Camporee

Hiking and Expedition

Drill and Marching

Special Events

Club Administration

Club Uniform

Fundraising

Innovative Practices

Challenges

The Future

Appendix

Preface

Adventurers and Pathfinders Living for Jesus provides a personal perception of the holistic purpose of the Adventurer and Pathfinder ministries based on my extensive experience as a parent, guardian, club Counsellor and Director. I have written this book from a pragmatic not a prescriptive perspective, recognising the different ways the ministries can be delivered and implemented.

The greatest gift any parent can give to their child is the love for Jesus. This is why Adventurer and Pathfinder clubs are more than a programme of marching, camping, curious hobbies, bugs and bats, they are ministries. The commitment to Kingdom living ultimately leads to building an ever-deeper relationship with the supreme Pathfinder Jesus Christ, our Lord and Saviour.

In writing this book, I deliberately chose the title "Living for Jesus" to emphasise the primary goal of the Adventurer and Pathfinder ministries. The book aims to help parents and their children to focus on gaining the best values for Kingdom living. I am a benefactor of the Adventurer and Pathfinder ministries, which formed the basis of my desire to accept Jesus Christ and become a baptised member of the worldwide Adventist Church. I have been honoured and privileged to serve the church as a club Counsellor, Director, Elder and Sponsor in both ministries. I now share these invaluable experiences with would-be club members and their parents and guardians, so they too can experience the full joy of living and serving for Jesus, the Master.

In this book, I plan to share my own experience leading young people in Adventurer and Pathfinder ministries, looking at what worked well and learning from what didn't work that well. I know that the Adventurer and Pathfinder ministries will differ in their delivery and implementation in different countries and continents but one thing I know is the universality of the aims and purpose of these ministries. I have included what I learned as a parent of three young children who I have guided through these ministries.

I plan to give all those involved in the Adventurer and Pathfinder ministries a blue print to their successful delivery and implementation. My passion of leading young people to Jesus Christ lends me to conclude that there is indeed nothing better than to live for Jesus.

Dr Mandela Thyoka

Introduction

The Adventurer and Pathfinder clubs are youth ministries within the Seventh-day Adventist Church that provide a holistic approach to the development of both children and adolescents through a range of activities and experiences. These clubs seek to help young people develop a strong sense of identity, belonging, and purpose within their community and their faith.

The Adventurer club is open to any children aged 4-9 years old, even children who are not Adventists. This club is a forerunner of the Pathfinder club, which enrols young people aged 10-15 years old. Both clubs offer a wide variety of activities, including outdoor adventures, community service projects, leadership development, and religious education. One of the key goals of these clubs is to help young people grow in their faith and develop a strong connection with their church and their community. The delivery of the curriculum is specific to the needs and ages of the children in both clubs, ultimately providing a nurturing environment where children can learn about God, develop a love for nature and serving others, and participate in fun and educational activities. The children undergo complete development of their physical, mental, and spiritual skills through a variety of activities such as camping, nature exploration, community service projects, and Bible study.

There is a strong emphasis on developing strong moral character, leadership skills, and a commitment to serving others from a very young age. In these clubs, children are provided a sense of community and belonging, offering a supportive environment where they can make friends, develop their interests, and deepen their faith. Each club is led by a team of dedicated adult leaders who are committed to helping young people grow and develop in a safe and supportive environment, ultimately giving the children and young people opportunities to form strong, positive relationships with their peers and adult mentors.

One of the most important aspects of Adventurer and Pathfinder clubs is their focus on family involvement. These clubs encourage parents to be actively involved in their children's club activities, which helps to strengthen family bonds and create a supportive network for young people as they navigate the challenges of adolescence.

Overall, Adventurer and Pathfinder clubs are an invaluable resource for the children and young people, providing them with a sense of belonging, purpose, and community, and help them grow and develop in their faith. This is a platform for young people to explore new skills and interests, form positive relationships, and develop leadership abilities. The clubs play a vital role in nurturing the next generation of Seventh-day Adventist leaders and community members.

Why living for Jesus?

Living for Jesus is more than an adage. Sin entered our world when our first parents fell from grace in the Garden of Eden (Genesis 3), and ever since humanity has been plagued by sin. Jesus was born to identify Himself with humanity, to save us from our sin (John 3:16). However, His incarnation (John 1) was only the first step in the ladder bridging humanity with heaven. Jesus spent His time on earth living a life of obedience to God, showing us an example to follow. At the end of His ministry here on earth, He became obedient to death (Philippians 2: 5-8), His death on the cross, a result of taking upon Himself all the sin of the world (2 Corinthians 5: 21) and becoming a substitute for our death. His resurrection conquered death, and He ascended to heaven after giving us the promise of the Holy Spirit, who He said would convict us of sin, righteousness, and judgement, granting us the power to live a sanctified life while we await His second advent, when Jesus returns to take His loved ones (John 14: 1-3).

So, since we have all sinned and fall short of the glory of God (Romans 3:23), we deserve to die as the wages of sin is death (Romans 6:23). But the vicarious death of Christ on Calvary and His subsequent resurrection grants all those who believe in Him the gift of salvation. We are saved by His grace through our faith, and the life we live we walk not by sight but by faith (Ephesians 2:8 – 10; Romans 1:17).

Living for Jesus is in recognition that we are not our own but that we belong to Him, bought at a price (1 Corinthians 6:19, 20). The Holy Spirit lives in us, and our lives are the fruit of the Spirit: love, joy, peace, long suffering etc. Jesus invites us to be perfect as our Father in Heaven is perfect, so living for Jesus means living as Jesus would want us to.

There is surely nothing better than living for Jesus. As the children progress through the Adventurer and Pathfinder ministries, the most important part of their development is to lead them to Jesus, our Saviour and Lord. When they come to know Jesus for themselves, they will learn from Him, and will become His disciples, and through their lifestyle, become His witnesses.

The Beginnings

The Seventh-day Adventist Pathfinder ministry is steeped in rich history that spans from the very humble beginnings to its growth and expansion into a worldwide movement, so much that the Pathfinder clubs now play a significant role in the development of young people within the Seventh-day Adventist community.

Let us consider the history in two parts: the early history (1907 to 1950) and the more recent history (1950 and beyond). The year 1950 provides a natural watershed moment when the General Conference of the Seventh-day Adventist Church allowed Pathfinder clubs to use world field Pathfinder Staff Training Course and How to Start a Pathfinder Club booklet.

The first Young People's Society was organised in 1879 before Ellen G White's call for specialised work for the youth in 1892. However, it was not until the turn of the century when the Missionary Volunteer (MV) and Junior Missionary Volunteer (JMV) societies were organised in 1907 and 1909 respectively. The pre-JMV classes of Busy Bee, Sun Beam, Builder and Helping Hand were developed in 1930 while JMV progressive classes of Friend and Companion were introduced in 1922. The Pathfinder name was first used at a summer camp in California in 1929. John H. Hancock designed the Pathfinder Club emblem in 1946, Helen Hobbs designed and made the Pathfinder flag in 1948 and Henry Bergh wrote the Pathfinder song in 1949. It was in 1950 that the General Conference authorised JMV Pathfinder clubs for world field and the Pathfinder Staff Training Course, How to Start a Pathfinder Club booklet and the Explorer class were also added.

In 1951, the Master Comrade was changed to Master Guide and the Pathfinder Staff Manual was published. The first local Area Pathfinder Camporee was held in 1951 in California, the first Union level Camporee was held in Lone Pine, California in 1960 and the first Division level Camporee was held at Camp Hale, Colorado, in 1985, with an attendance of 16,129. The Pioneer class which was established in 1966 became known as Ranger in 1970 and the Voyager class was added in 1982. The first ever International Pathfinder Camporee, 'Dare to Care', was held in Denver, Colorado, in 1994, with an attendance of 12,300, followed by subsequent International Camporees - the 1999 'Discover the Power' Camporee in Oshkosh, Wisconsin, with an attendance of over 20,000, the 2004 'Faith on Fire' Camporee held in Oshkosh, Wisconsin, with an attendance of 31,000 from 83 countries, the 2009 'Courage to Stand' Camporee held in Oshkosh, Wisconsin, with an attendance of over 36,000, the 2014 'Forever Faithful' Camporee held in Oshkosh, Wisconsin, with an attendance of over 46,000 from 50 countries and the 2019 'Chosen' Camporee held in Oshkosh, Wisconsin, with an attendance of about 55,000 from 92 countries. The next one 'Believe the Promise' is due to be held in Gillette, Wyoming in 2024.

The Adventurer programme became an independent programme from Pathfinders in 1989. The Teen Leadership Training (TLT) programme was established for training High school students in 1995, the same year the first Pathfinder website was launched. The Adventurer programme, which was an offshoot from the main Pathfinder programme, was created for parents to assist them in their important responsibilities as a child's primary teachers and evangelists. The ultimate purpose was to strengthen the parent/child relationship and optimise the child's development in spiritual, physical, mental, and social areas. The family, church and school were to work together to develop a mature and a happy child.

The General Conference endorsed the idea of the Adventurer classes of Busy Bee, Sunbeam, Builder, and

Helping Hand in 1939 and Adventurer club, which was piloted in 1990 became a fully-fledged programme in 1992 after it was developed by child specialists into age-appropriate curriculum and awards.

At first glance, you would have been excused for thinking that the Adventurer and Pathfinder ministries of today have always been the way they are. The history of these clubs is one of passion, dedication, and a commitment to nurturing the next generation of faithful and responsible individuals. In studying their origins, we can understand how to remain true to the original goals that early pioneers had in mind when developing these ministries.

How to start your own club

It may seem very daunting at first, but starting a new club should not be so. In fact, using some simple guidelines, one can make the task manageable. So, what are some steps that I recommend when planning to start your own club?

Firstly, gather interest from would-be Adventurers, Pathfinders and their parents and guardians. The interest stems from attending and watching other clubs at work, either during club activities or special programmes such as induction or investiture ceremonies. Identify a parent or guardian with a strong passion for Adventurers and Pathfinders to be an ideal candidate for leading a new club. It is not always necessary for the leader to be a Master Guide, however helpful this may be, but that the leader should show commitment to the cause. In due time, enrolment into a Master Guide or Pathfinder Leadership Award would provide the full armamentarium for the new leader.

In my experience of helping to start two new clubs, the most important part that proved pivotal to the successful launching of the clubs was the interest of the parents or guardians. I strongly believe that without their interest, support and commitment, all our efforts would have come to nothing. I remember in my very first meetings with the parents and guardians when I alluded to the fact that as their leader, I would match the same level of commitment that they offer to the club. This meant that when they give their child and the club one hundred percent support, I would also match that level of commitment.

One of the major challenges that many new clubs face is the lack of club Counsellors and/or leaders. I have often encouraged parents or guardians to become club Counsellors and to take up various roles within the club.

They already know the children, they have vested interest in seeing them grow, and so it is so vital for the club's early success when they become part of the club. Once you have garnered interest from parents and guardians, the next step is to get interest from the church and her leadership. You will need to gain permission from the church board, who will endorse the need to start a new club, approving the checks and balances needed to get the club registered with the local Conference. A vote may need to be passed by the board, followed by a subsequent letter (with the board minutes) circulated to the local Conference informing them of the new club. The local Conference, through the Pathfinder Department will then provide the support and guidance to the new club ranging from registering the club, getting club insurance for the club activities, arranging for safeguarding training for club staff and leaders and further providing the new club with an annual calendar of events as a starting point.

Once registered, the new club can then plan a local calendar of events based on the Conference's events, especially noting two important dates - club induction and club investiture. The club induction allows for the official recognition of the club by the church and the community, opening the club to children who will abide by the club's pledge and law. It is during the club's induction service that community leaders such as Local Councillors and Member(s) of Parliament and the Civic Mayor may be invited to attend and provide the much-needed connection with the community.

At this juncture, the new club will then seek to have a budget for its planned activities for the year, focusing on fundraising ventures that will add to the church board's allocated budget. I believe that clubs who prosper have a dedicated fundraising team that will constantly seek to look at channels of fundraising platforms and ideas, while the leadership provides the much-needed vision for the club.

Some funds are best recovered from the children's enrolment or registration fee, commonly set as a fixed fee for the whole year, following consideration of the costs of running the club, such as the purchase of activity workbooks.

As the new club takes root, constant vigilance is required to keep the club focused on the primary task of leading young souls to Christ. Constant reviews, reflection and assessments help to develop best practices, even learning from best practices of sister clubs. The church is kept abreast of further progress of the new club through having special days such as Adventurer and Pathfinder Days, helping gain further interest and momentum.

My Memoirs

I was privileged to be asked to help start a new Pathfinder club at our sister church in South Yorkshire, United Kingdom. The invitation came from the parents themselves through our Church Pastor, who was serving our District of churches. The first thing I did was to pray about the request and seek guidance from the Lord, then together with my wife and children, we committed to pray about the request, waiting on the Lord's answer. It wasn't long, our wait was over after a few sessions of prayer, when the Lord revealed His plan for this ministry.

The church board was then advised of my role, as a facilitator, being the Elder and Sponsor of the Pathfinder club at my local church. I happily met with the parents and the Head Elder of our sister Church. At that meeting we identified one of the parents as the point of contact and de facto Director of this new club. We chose a local parent to make sure that the club would carry on meeting way beyond my term of reference.

This first meeting provided me an opportunity to share with the parents the structure of the Adventurer and

Pathfinder ministries. One of the parents, with prior permission, obtained a full list of the names of the children who were being considered to join this new club. We contacted the local Conference Youth department to introduce the club and obtain insurance for the club.

Policies for safeguarding, keeping the church family safe and club discipline were instituted and adopted for use. The club started to meet when the minimum set of mandatory requirements were met. We continued to grow in numbers, carrying on with curriculum work in the workbooks and joining with our sister club, wherever possible, for joint and Conference-wide events.

When I finished my tenure after two years, the club was self-sustaining and continuing to make good progress. On reflection, the club continued to grow because of the interest of the local parents, who then made sure that the club got all the support it needed.

Adventurer Programme

The Adventurer clubs are fun clubs created for children aged between 4 and 9 years old and currently serve more than one million kids around the world. The clubs specialise in weekly activities that meet the psychological needs of this age group and affording parents the opportunities for learning parenting skills and enjoying special activities with their children. The club works best when parents/guardians work with their child in the activities and assignments. These range from games and outdoor activities to nature exploration and family camping, field trips and community service projects, along with approximately 80 specialised award areas of crafts, nature, recreation, spiritual development and home arts.

Adventurer Pledge
Because Jesus loves me, I will always do my best.

Adventurer Law
Be obedient
Be pure
Be true
Be kind
Be respectful
Be attentive
Be helpful
Be cheerful
Be thoughtful
Be reverent

Adventurer Song
We are Adventurers,
At home, at school, at play.
We are Adventurers,
We're learning every day
To be honest, kind, and true,
To be like Jesus through and through!
We are Adventurers!

Adventurer Classes
The curriculum requirements for each of the Adventurer classes are divided into five separate tracks, a general or basic requirement section and four other sections namely My God, My Self, My Family and My World, as related to the Adventurer child.

It is very important to register children in the Adventurer programme as early as possible, so that they can start at the beginning of the programme and work their way through each of the classes, building on previous class's work. However, care is taken to place each child in the age-appropriate class, matching with their development.

Adventurer Class Structure

Class	Age/School year
Little Lamb	4 years/Pre-school
Early Bird	5 years/Reception
Busy Bee	6 years/Year 1 or Grade 1
Sunbeam	7 years/Year 2 or Grade 2
Builder	8 years/Year 3 or Grade 3
Helping hand	9 years/Year 4 or Grade 4

Little Lamb

General requirement stipulates that one must be 4 years old and/or in Preschool/Pre-kindergarten or its equivalent and be an active member of the Adventurer Club. The essence of this class is four-fold, namely, to demonstrate God's love for children, to promote the values expressed in the Adventurer Pledge and Song, to create an environment where all children can contribute and to encourage children to have fun. There is no strict entry age for this class, with any child under the age of 4 years eligible to enrol. If a child enrols in this class at a very early age, they can remain in this class until eligible to graduate to the mainstream Adventurer classes.

The main basic requirement is for children to recite the Adventurer Pledge and sing "Jesus is My Shepherd".

Little Lambs learn about God through singing a song about Jesus, listening to a story about Jesus, saying three things they've learned about Jesus, making a craft about Jesus, completing an activity about Jesus and completing two stars - Woolly Lamb and Little boy Jesus. Some of these requirements can be fulfilled during the Sabbath School lessons. In learning about themselves, Little Lambs do this by singing a song about their body, listening to a story about the body, saying three things they've learned about their bodies, making a craft about bodies, completing an activity about bodies and completing two stars named Sharing and Healthy Foods. Little Lambs learn about their families by singing a song about families, listening to a story about families, saying three things they've learned about families, making a craft about families, completing an activity about families and completing two stars, namely Special Helper star and Healthy Me. Lastly, Little Lambs learn about their world through singing a song about creation, listening to a story about creation, saying three things they've learned about creation, making a craft about creation, completing an activity about creation and completing two stars, My Friend Jesus and Community Helpers. There are additional stars they can earn, depending on their progress.

Early Bird

General requirement stipulates that one must be 5 years old and/or in Reception/Kindergarten or its equivalent and be an active member of the Adventurer Club. The main goals for this class are to demonstrate God's love for children, to promote the values expressed in the Adventurer Pledge and Law, to create an environment where all children can contribute and to encourage children to have fun.

The main basic requirement in this class is for children to recite the Adventurer Pledge, recite their country's Pledge of Allegiance or national anthem and pray independently.

Early Birds learn about God by learning the fourth commandment: "Remember the Sabbath day, to keep it holy" (Exodus 20:8) and completing the Beavers, Bible friends and God's world chips. In learning about self, Early Birds complete the Alphabet, Manners Fun and Know Your Body chips. Early Birds learn about their family by memorising the fifth commandment: "honour your father and your mother" (Exodus 20:12) and completing Fire Safety, Helping at Home chip, and Pets/Toys chips. Lastly, Early Birds learn about their world by completing My Community Friends, Playing with Friends and the Scavenger Hunt chips, with further additional chips available to those showing very good progress.

Busy Bee

General requirement stipulates that one must be 6 years old and/or in Year 1/Grade1 or its equivalent and be an active member of the Adventurer Club. The four main goals in this class are to demonstrate God's love for children, to promote the values expressed in the Adventurer Pledge and Law, to create an environment where all children can contribute and to encourage children to have fun.

Firstly, the basic requirements are to recite and accept the Adventurer Pledge and complete the Busy Bee Reading award.

Busy Bees learn about God by learning God's plan to save them by creating a story chart or lapbook showing the order in which these events took place (from creation, the first sin, how Jesus cares for us today, Jesus promise to come again and heaven) and using the story chart to show someone how much Jesus cares for them. They also learn about God's message to them by completing the Bible I award and God's power in their lives by spending regular quiet time with Jesus to talk with Him and learn about Him and asking three people why they pray. A key area of learning about self is knowing that they are special by participating in an activity or making a craft showing different people who care for them and that they can make wise decisions by learning at least four different feelings and participating in an activity or making a craft showing different feelings. Busy bees then complete the Health Specialist award to show that they can care for their bodies. Children learn that each one of us has a family and they can show or explain what they like about each family member and how family members care for each other. They also discover what the fifth commandment (Exodus 20:12) tells them about families by acting out three ways they can honour their own family. Lastly the children learn how their family helps them care for themselves by completing the Safety Specialist award. Regarding their world, Busy Bees tell how they can be a good friend to others using puppets, role playing or any method of their choice, they also discuss the work people do for their church by learning about one job by helping the person do it. Lastly, Busy Bees discuss the world of nature by completing the Friend of Animals award, with additional awards available to those achieving highly.

Sunbeam

General requirement stipulates that one must be 7 years old and/or in Year 2/Grade 2 or its equivalent and be an active member of the Adventurer Club. In relation to the Sunbeam class, the main goals are to demonstrate God's love for children, to promote the values expressed in the Adventurer Pledge and Law, to create an environment where all children can contribute and to encourage children to have fun.

The basic investiture requirements are to recite and accept the Adventurer Law and to complete the Sunbeam Reading award.

Children in the Sunbeam class learn about God's plan to save them by creating a story chart or lapbook showing Jesus' birth, life, death and resurrection and they use their story chart or lapbook to show someone the joy of being saved by Jesus. They also learn about God's Message to them by memorising and explaining two Bible verses about being saved by Jesus (Matthew 22:37-39, 1 John 1:9, Isaiah 1:18, Romans 6:23, or any verse of their choice). They learn to name the two major parts of the Bible and the four gospels, complete the Friend of Jesus award and learn about God's Power in their lives by spending regular quiet time with Jesus to talk with Him and learn about Him and asking three people why they study the Bible. Sunbeams learn that they are special by making a tracing of themselves, decorating it with pictures and words which tell good things about themselves. They also demonstrate that they can make wise choices by participating in an activity about choices and that they can care for their body by completing the Fitness Fun award. In learning about their family, Sunbeams create a family collage, scrapbook, crest, or coat of arms and show how family members care for each other and how Jesus can help them deal with disagreements by using puppets, role play or any method of their choice. In showing how their family helps them care for themselves the Sunbeams complete the Road Safety award. In nature, Sunbeams explore their neighbourhood to list things that are good and things they could make better and from that list they choose ways and spend time making their neighbourhood a better place. They complete the Courtesy award to learn about their world of friends and complete the Friend of Nature award to learn about the world of nature. The additional awards can then be taken by those who have achieved highly.

Builder

General requirement stipulates that one must be 8 years old and/or in Year 3/Grade 3 or its equivalent and be an active member of the Adventurer Club. The main goals in the Builder class are to demonstrate God's love for children, to promote the values expressed in the Adventurer Pledge and Law, to create an environment where all children can contribute and to encourage children to have fun.

The Builder basic investiture requirements are to recite the Adventurer Pledge and Law, to explain the Pledge and to complete the Builder Reading award.

Builders learn about God's plan to save them by creating a story chart or lapbook showing the order in which these stories took place such as Paul - The disciples share Jesus' love, Martin Luther - God's church obeys, Ellen White - God's church prepares for His coming and about the Builder themselves - I get ready to meet Jesus) and then use this story chart or lapbook to show someone how to give their life to Jesus. They also learn of God's message to them by finding, memorising and explaining three Bible verses about giving one's life to Jesus such as Acts 16:31, John 1:12, Galatians 3:26, 2 Corinthians 5:17, Psalm 51:10 or a text of their choice. Builders also learn to name the books of the New Testament and learn about God's power in their lives by spending a regular quiet time with Jesus to talk with Him and learn about Him and completing the Prayer award. The builders learn that they are special by putting together a scrapbook, poster, or collage, showing some things they can do to serve God and others. They learn how they make wise choices by participating in an activity that shows the results of good and bad decisions and completing the Media Critic Award. On the other hand, they learn how to take care of their own body by completing the Temperance Award. Builders learn that they have a family by creating a family flag or banner or making a collage of stories and/or photographs about their family. They are encouraged to find a story in the Bible about a family that changed and to learn how their family cares for each other by playing a game by having each family member show appreciation to each of the other members of the family. Lastly, they learn how their family helps them care for themselves when they complete the Wise Steward Award. Regarding their world of friends, other people and nature, Builders learn to make friends with a person of another culture or generation, or someone who has a disability and invite that person to a family or church event, know and explain their national anthem and flag and name their country's capital, and the leader of their country and complete an award for nature, not previously earned. For those completing successfully, there are also additional awards to choose to complete.

Helping Hand

General requirement stipulates that one must be 9 years old and/or in Year 4/Grade 4 or its equivalent and be an active member of the Adventurer Club. In the Helping Hand, the main goals are to demonstrate God's love for children, to promote the values expressed in the Adventurer Pledge and Law, to create an environment where all children can contribute and to encourage children to have fun.

The basic Helping Hand investiture requirements are to recite the Adventurer Pledge and Law, to explain the Law and to complete the Helping Hand Reading award.

Children in this class learn about God's plan to save them by creating a story chart or lapbook showing the order in which these stories took place: Noah - Water cleans the earth, Abraham - God calls a people, Moses - A promised land for God's people, David - God works with His people and Daniel - God's people disobey, then they use this story chart or lapbook to show someone how to live for God. They also learn about God's power in their lives by spending regular quiet time with Jesus to talk with Him and learn about Him and journaling their time by writing, drawing, or recording a video. With an adult, they then choose one thing in their life which Jesus has promised to help them improve. Lastly, they complete the Bible II award about God's message to them.

Helping Hand class learn that they are special by listing some special interests and abilities God has given them and by sharing about their talents in a talent show or a show and tell. They learn the steps of good decision-making and use them to solve two real-life problems, to show that they can make wise choices. By completing the Hygiene award, they show evidence that they can care for their own body. The class learns that each one of us has a family by making a scrapbook or picture book about their family history. They help plan a special family worship, family night, or family outing to show that family members care for each other and complete a level 3 or 4 award not previously earned to show that their family helps them to care for themselves. By completing the Caring Friend, the Country Fun and the Environmentalist awards, the class fulfils the world of friends, other people and nature.

Helping hand represents the last of the Adventurer progressive achievement classes, at which time the graduate is ready to enrol in the Pathfinder programme.

Adventurer Awards

The Adventurer club Awards programme is an important aspect of the Adventurer ministry, designed to recognise and reward the achievements of its young members. The Adventurer club seeks to provide a holistic and nurturing environment for children, fostering their physical, mental, and spiritual growth. The award system plays a crucial role in this mission, motivating young Adventurers to actively participate in club activities and strive for personal development. There are more than 150 Adventurer Stars, Chips, and Awards available for completion, in the following six levels: Little Lamb, Eager Beaver, Busy Bee, Sunbeam, Builder, and Helping Hand (see Appendix B). Some of these are multi-level and others are special award badges.

The programme consists of various awards and badges that Adventurers can earn as they progress through the club. These awards are generally divided into different categories, each representing a specific area of growth and accomplishment. Among the most common categories are nature, outdoor skills, music, personal growth, and service. Each category has its own set of requirements and challenges, encouraging Adventurers to explore different interests and talents as they work towards earning their awards.

One of the key benefits of the Adventurer club awards is the opportunity for children to set and achieve personal goals. By earning awards, Adventurers gain a sense of accomplishment and pride in their abilities. This, in turn, helps to boost their self-confidence and self-esteem, paving the way for continued personal growth and success. Furthermore, the process of working towards awards teaches children important life skills such as perseverance, goal setting, and time management.

In addition to personal development, the award programme also fosters a sense of camaraderie among club members. As Adventurers work on earning their awards, they often collaborate with their peers, learning to communicate effectively and work as part of a team. This not only strengthens their relationships with their fellow club members but also helps to foster a spirit of cooperation and unity within the club.

Furthermore, the Adventurer club awards serve as a valuable tool for parents and club leaders to track the progress and achievements of their young members. By earning awards, children demonstrate their dedication and commitment to the club, and it also highlights their individual strengths and interests. This allows parents and leaders to better understand and support the development of each Adventurer, helping them to provide personalised guidance and encouragement.

Adventurer club awards are a great way to recognise the hard work and dedication of the young members of the club. These awards are designed to give children a sense of accomplishment and to motivate them to continue their involvement in the club. There are a variety of awards that can be earned in Adventurer club, each one representing different skills and achievements.

One of the most popular awards in Adventurer club is the Basic level award. This award is typically earned by completing a series of requirements that are designed to help children learn important life skills and build character. These requirements may include learning about safety and first aid, participating in community service projects, and completing outdoor activities. By earning the Basic level award, children can demonstrate their ability to take on new challenges and work well with others.

In addition to the Basic level award, there are also more specialised awards that children can earn in Adventurer club. For example, the Nature award recognises children who have shown an interest in and knowledge of the natural world. This award may require children to complete activities such as bird watching, nature hikes, and plant identification. By earning the Nature award, children can demonstrate their appreciation for the environment and their willingness to learn about the world around them.

Another popular award in Adventurer club is the Camping award. This award is earned by completing a series of camping-related activities, such as setting up a tent, cooking over a fire, and learning how to navigate in the wilderness. By earning the Camping award, children can demonstrate their ability to be self-sufficient and comfortable in outdoor settings.

Overall, Adventurer club awards are a great way to recognise the achievements of young club members and to motivate them to continue their involvement in the club. These awards are designed to be challenging but achievable, giving children the opportunity to develop new skills and build character. By earning these awards, children can demonstrate their dedication and commitment to the club, and to their own personal growth.

Pathfinder Programme

Pathfinder programme is designed for children ages 10-15 and accepts any youth who promises to abide by the Pathfinder Pledge and Law regardless of their church affiliation. The ministry has now reached nearly 2 million members around the world.

Pathfinder aim
The Advent Message to all the world in my generation.

Pathfinder Motto
The love of Christ compels us.

Pathfinder Pledge
By the grace of God,
I will be pure and kind and true.
I will keep the Pathfinder Law.
I will be a servant of God
and a friend to man.

Pathfinder Law
The Pathfinder Law is for me to:
Keep the morning watch.
Do my honest part.
Care for my body.
Keep a level eye.
Be courteous and obedient.
Walk softly in the sanctuary.
Keep a song in my heart.
Go on God's errands.

Pathfinder Song
Oh, we are the Pathfinders strong,
The servants of God are we.
Faithful as we march along,
In kindness, truth, and purity
A Message to tell to the world,
A truth that will set us free!
King Jesus the Saviour's coming back
For you, and me!

Pathfinder Classes
Pathfinder classes have general requirements that specify the age and/or grade or year of school study and requires one to be an active member of the Pathfinder club. The other areas of the curriculum focus on spiritual discovery, serving others, friendship development, health and fitness, organisation and leadership development and nature study and outdoor life.

Pathfinder Class Structure

Class	Age/School year
Friend	10 years/Year 6 or Grade 5
Companion	11 years/Year 7 or Grade 6
Explorer	12 years/Year 8 or Grade 7
Ranger	13 years/Year 9 or Grade 8
Voyager	14 years/Year 10 or Grade 9
Guide	15 years/Year 11 or Grade 11

Friend
General requirement stipulates that one must be 10 years old and/or in Year 6/Grade 5 or its equivalent and be an active member of the Pathfinder Club. Class members read the book "The Happy Path", a book on the Pledge and Law by Lawrence Maxwell, helping them memorise and explain

the Pathfinder Pledge and Law. Several books are also included in the Book club certificate. An advanced requirement is to know, sing or play, and explain the meaning of the Pathfinder Song.

Spiritual discovery includes memorising the Old Testament (OT) books of the Bible and knowing the five areas into which the OT books are grouped and demonstrating an ability to find any given book. Friend class should also hold a current memory gem certificate involving at least seven texts committed to memory and should know and explain one of the two large passages - Psalm 23 or Psalm 46. Further work involves completing a crossword puzzle based on the prologue to Early Writings and group discussion of how Christ's loving care and deliverance are shown in the story of one of these Old Testament characters: Joseph, Jonah, Esther or Ruth. At home, children are encouraged to read with their parents the historical prologue to the book Early Writings and list the main events of the SDA church during several worship periods.

To demonstrate serving others, friend class members work out ways to spend at least two hours expressing their friendship to someone in need in their community by either visiting someone who needs friendship or helping someone in need. With the help of others, the class member spends a half day on a community, school, or church project, proving a good citizen at home and at school. This culminates in bringing at least two visitors to Sabbath School or Pathfinder meetings.

On friendship, the children list ten qualities of being a good friend and discuss four everyday situations where they may have practiced the "Golden Rule." Secondly, they should know their National Anthem and explain its meaning. Lastly, they should demonstrate good table manners with a group of persons of various ages.

In terms of health and fitness, they are required to discuss the temperance principles in the life of Daniel or participate in a presentation or role play on Daniel 1, memorise and explain Daniel 1:8, and either sign the appropriate pledge card or design their own pledge card showing why they choose a lifestyle in harmony with the true principles of temperance. They are required to learn the principles of a healthful diet and engage in a project preparing a chart of basic food groups, complete the honour in Beginner's Swimming and learn the HIV/AIDS curriculum.

For organisation and leadership development, the friend class members plan and take a three hour or 8 km hike and complete a requirement under the Nature Study or Outdoor Life sections or a Nature Honour.

In nature study, they can complete one of the following honours: Cats, Dogs, Mammals, Seeds, Bird Pets and know different methods of purifying water and demonstrate their ability to build a camp shelter. The spiritual meaning of this is to consider the significance of Jesus as the water of life and as our refuge place. Those who may wish to gain advance requirements should know and identify ten wild flowers and ten insects in your area.

The outdoor life requires practical learning, knowing how ropes are made and demonstrating how to care for rope in the correct manner. They are required to tie and know the practical use of the following knots: Overhand, Granny, Square, Slip, Double Bow, Two Half Hitches, Clove Hitch, Bowline. One major requirement is to participate in an overnight campout during which time they can pass a test in general safety, learn to pitch and strike a tent and make a camp bed. Similarly, they should know ten hiking rules, and know what to do when lost, learn the signs for track and trail and to lay a 2km trail that others can follow and track. Other outdoor skills to learn include starting a fire with one match, using natural materials, and keeping that fire going.

Those pathfinders aiming for advanced requirements can then learn how to properly use the knife and axe, and know ten safety rules in their use, learn to tie five speed knots, demonstrate baking, boiling and frying camp food and complete one honour in Arts and Crafts, Vocational or Outdoor Industries.

Companion

One must be 11 years old and/or in Year 7/Grade 6 or its equivalent, and an active member of the Pathfinder Club. They should read the book "The Happy Path" or a similar book on the Pledge and Law if not previously read, learn or review the meaning of the Pathfinder Pledge and illustrate its meaning in an interesting way, have a current Book Club Certificate and write at least a paragraph of review on one book of their choice and in advanced cases only, know the composition and proper use of your National Flag.

The Spiritual discovery includes memorising the New Testament books and knowing the four areas into which the books are grouped and demonstrating one's ability to find any given book. The Pathfinders should hold a current memory gem certificate on areas such as. They should show their knowledge of what Christ taught in one of the following ways, Christ's Parables, Christ's Miracles, Sermon on the Mount or Second Advent Sermon and read the gospels of Matthew and Mark in any translation.

In serving others, children in this class work out ways to spend at least two hours in their community demonstrating in a consistent manner, real companionship to someone else and spend at least a half day participating in a project that will benefit the community or their church. For advanced requirements, they may participate in an outreach activity, and bring a non-SDA friend to participate or observe and discuss the principle and demonstrate the meaning of respect for people of different cultures and gender and also demonstrate respect for their parents/guardian and what they provide for them.

To achieve health and fitness requirements, the pathfinders memorise and explain 1 Corinthians 9:24-27 and discuss physical fitness and regular exercise as they relate to healthful living, learning about the detrimental effects of smoking on health and fitness, and writing one's own pledge of commitment to abstaining from the use of tobacco. In advanced cases, they complete the Advanced Beginner's Swimming honour, study the HIV/AIDS curriculum and attend a five-day Plan, or view two films on health, or make a poster on smoking or drug abuse, or help prepare a display on tobacco for a show.

To meet the organisation and leadership requirement, the pathfinder plans and leads a devotional service for their group, helping their Unit or Club plan a special activity such as a party, hike, or overnight campout. In advanced cases, they can participate in a special club event such as an Investiture, open house, induction, or Pathfinder Sabbath and then evaluate the event to determine how it can be improved.

For nature study, they can participate in nature games or participate in a one-hour nature walk and then complete one of the following honours: Amphibians, Birds, Livestock, Poultry, Reptiles, Shells, Trees, or Shrubs. They also review the study of creation and keep a seven-day outdoor log of their personal observations from nature in which each day focuses on those parts that were created on that day and in advanced cases only, they identify and describe twelve birds in the wild and twelve native trees.

Outdoor life includes learning to find the eight general directions without the aid of a compass, participating in a two-night campout and knowing at least 6 points relative to the selection of a campsite. They continually learn or review the knots in Friend class and learn to tie and know the practical use of the following knots: Sheet Bend,

Sheepshank, Fisherman's Knot, Timber Hitch, Taut Line Hitch and pass a test in Companion first aid. In those aiming for advanced requirements, they can learn to build five different fires and describe their uses, discuss the safety rules in lighting fires, or undertake an 8km hike and keep a log, cook a camp meal without utensils or prepare a knot board with at least fifteen different knots. This can be complemented with one honour in Arts and Crafts not previously earned, and honours in Household Arts, Health & Science, Vocational, or Outdoor Industries not previously earned.

Explorer

An explorer must be 12 years old and/or in Year 8/ Grade 7 or its equivalent and be an active member of the Pathfinder Club. They will learn or review the meaning of the Pathfinder Law and demonstrate their understanding by participating in one of the following: role play, panel discussion, essay, or prepare a project of their choice. They should read the book "The Happy Path" if not previously read and have a current Book Club Certificate and write at least a paragraph of review on each book. If advanced, they should know the composition and proper use of the Pathfinder Flag and Unit Guidon.

For spiritual discovery, they should become familiar with the use of a concordance and hold a current memory gem certificate. They are required to read the gospels Luke and John in any translation, and discuss in their group any three of the following: Luke 4:16-19 - The Scripture Reading, Luke 11:9-13 - Ask, Seek, Knock, Luke 21:25-28 - Signs of Second Coming, John 13:12-17 - Humility, John 14:1-3 - Lord's Promise or John 15:5-8 - Vine and Branches). Also, they should choose any one of the following passages: John 3 - Nicodemus, John 4 - The Woman at the Well, Luke 15 - The Prodigal Son, Luke 10 -

The Good Samaritan or Luke 19 – Zacchaeus, and share their understanding of how Jesus saves individuals by using one of the following methods, group discussion with their leader, giving a talk, writing an essay, making a series of pictures, charts or models or writing a poem or song. They should also memorise and explain Proverbs 20:1 and Proverbs 23:29-32. If doing so for advanced requirements, they should read about J. N. Andrews and discuss the importance of mission service to the church and why Christ gave the Great Commission (Matthew 28: 18-20) and complete the map work on missionaries and places of service.

In serving others, an explorer should become familiar with the community services in their area and give assistance to at least one and participate in at least three church programmes. In advance requirements, they should enrol a new member in Sabbath School, Pathfinders, or Bible Correspondence Course.

For friendship development, they can participate in a panel discussion or skit or peer pressure and its role in their decision making and tour their municipal offices or have a city official visit their group and then explain 5 ways they can cooperate with them. In advance cases, they can earn one of the following honours, Christian grooming and manners and family life.

To achieve health and fitness requirements, explorers should complete one of the following two requirements: participate in a group discussion on the physical effects of the drug alcohol on the body, view an audio/visual on alcohol or other drugs, and discuss the effects on the human body or peer pressure discussion. In advanced cases, they can participate in a 16-km hike and make a list of clothing to be worn or undertake peer pressure and AIDS Awareness discussions.

For organisation and leadership development, an explorer can lead out in their club's opening exercises or a

Sabbath School programme or help their unit or club plan a special outreach activity such as a project for unfortunate children, community beautification, etc. and carry out the activity. If doing advanced requirements, they can participate in a special club event such as an Investiture, open house, induction, Pathfinder Sabbath, etc. and participate in the evaluation of the event afterwards along with the Companion Class.

For nature study, if an explorer lives in the Northern Hemisphere, they should be able to identify the North Star, Orion, Pleiades, and two planets, however, if they live in the Southern Hemisphere, identify Achernar, The Southern Cross, Centaurus, and Orion and know the spiritual significance of Orion as told in Early Writings. They complete one of the following honours: Animal Tracking, Cacti, Flowers, Stars, or Weather and identify six tracks of animals or birds. Make a plaster cast of three tracks.

In outdoor life, they should participate in a two-night camp out, describe six points of a good campsite, plan and cook two meals and pass a test in Explorer first aid. They should be able to explain what a topographical map is, what you can expect to find on it, and its uses and identify at least twenty signs and symbols used on topographic maps. For advanced requirements, they can review the basic lashings and build one article of camp furniture, plan a menu for a three day camping trip for four people, using at least three different dehydrated foods and be able to send and receive the semaphore alphabet, be able to send and receive the international Morse code by wigwag, know the alphabet in sign language for the deaf, or have a basic knowledge of procedures of two-way radio communication. In lifestyle enrichment, an explorer completes one honour in Household Arts, or Arts and Crafts not previously earned, or for advanced requirements, completes one honour in Outreach Ministry, Health & Science, Vocational or Outdoor Industries, not previously earned.

Ranger

The basic requirement is for a ranger to be a teenager 13 years of age, and/or in Year 9/Grade 8 or its equivalent, be an active member of the Pathfinder Club and memorise and understand the Adventist Youth Aim and Motto. They should select and read three books of their choice from the teen Book Club List.

In spiritual discovery, using group discussion, they should discover what Christianity is, what the marks of a true disciple are, the forces involved in becoming a Christian, have a memory gem certificate, participate in a Bible marking programme on the inspiration of the Bible and enrol at least three people in a Bible Correspondence Course. They can complete the Christian Citizenship Honour if not previously done, participate at least once, in two different types of outreach programmes, with the help of a friend, spend a full day (at least 8 hours) working on a project for their church, school, or community. If doing advanced requirements, they should conduct two Bible studies with non-Seventh-day Adventists.

For friendship development, in a group discussion and by personal inquiry they should examine their attitudes to two of the following topics: self-confidence, the social graces, friendship or will power. They can role play the story of the Good Samaritan, and think of ways to serve three neighbours, and then do so to achieve advanced requirements.

In health and fitness, the ranger should participate in one of the following, either discuss the principles of physical fitness, provide an outline of their daily exercise programme and write out and sign a personal pledge of commitment to a regular exercise programme or discuss the natural advantages of living the Adventist Christian lifestyle in accordance with Biblical principles. In advanced requirements, they should participate in one of the following activities, hike 15km and keep a log, cycle 80 km, ride a horse 15 km, swim 1 km or go on a one-day canoe trip. They should discuss the concept, types and purpose of dating.

For organisation and leadership development, they should attend at least one church business meeting and prepare a brief report for discussion in your group. With their group, they should make plans for a social activity at least once a quarter. In advanced requirements only, they complete requirements 3 and 6 of the Drilling and Marching Honour if not previously done.

For nature study, a ranger reviews the story of the flood and studies at least three different fossils; explain their origin and relate them to breaking God's Law and then completes a Nature honour not previously earned. In advanced requirements, the ranger must be able to identify through photographs, sketches, pictures or real life, one of the following categories: 25 tree leaves; 25 rocks and minerals; 25 wild flowers; 25 butterflies and moths; 25 shells.

For outdoor living, they should build and demonstrate the use of a reflector oven by cooking something, participate in a two-night camp out and be able to pack a pack or rucksack, including personal gear and food sufficient for your participation in a two-night camp out and pass a test in Ranger first aid. In advanced requirements, a ranger completes the Orienteering honour and demonstrate that they can light a fire on a rainy day or in the snow, know where to get the dry material to keep it going and demonstrate ability to properly tighten and replace an axe handle. In lifestyle enrichment, a ranger completes one honour in Outreach Ministry, Vocational, or Outdoor Industries not previously earned or in advanced requirement, completes one honour in Recreation or Arts and Crafts, not previously earned.

Voyager

General requirement stipulates that one must be a teenager 14 years of age, and/or in Year 10/Grade 9 or its equivalent, be an active member of Pathfinders and through memorisation and discussion, explain the meaning of the Adventist Youth Pledge. They should also select and read three books of their choice from the Teen Book Club list, and in advanced requirements, they can make a written or oral presentation on respect for God's law and civil authority giving at least ten principles of moral behaviour.

In spiritual discovery, they study the personal work of the Holy Spirit as it relates to mankind, and discuss His involvement in spiritual growth. Also, by study and group discussion they increase their knowledge of the last-day events that lead up to the Second Advent, and discover the true meaning of Sabbath keeping. They should hold a current Memory Gem Certificate and in case of advanced requirements, read the books of Proverbs, Habakkuk, Isaiah, Malachi, Jeremiah or complete the Junior Bible Year reading programme.

In serving others, as a group or individually, they can invite a friend to at least one of their Church or Conference Teen/Youth Fellowship activities, help organise and participate in a project of service to others and discuss how a Christian Adventist youth relates to people in everyday situations, contacts and associations. In achieving advanced requirements, they should spend at least 2 hours with their Pastor, Church Elder or Deacon observing them in their pastoral/care ministry.

For friendship development, in a group discussion and by personal inquiry examine their attitudes toward two of the following topics: self-concept, human relationships (parents, family, and others), earning and spending money or peer pressure. They should list and discuss the needs of the handicapped and help plan and participate in a party for them and in advanced requirements, they can visit an institute for physically or mentally challenged and present a report on the visit.

In health and fitness, they can choose and complete any two requirements from the Temperance honour, organize a Health Party to include health principles, talks, displays, etc. In aiming for advanced requirements, they can study the effective refusal technique of Joseph and explain why it is important to use it today.

For organisation and leadership development, the Voyager prepares and discusses a flow chart on local Church organisation and lists the departmental functions, participate in local church programs on two occasions each, in two departments of the church and fulfil requirements 3, 5, and 6 of the Stewardship honour and complete the Drilling and Marching honour and, for advanced requirement only, the Junior Youth Witnessing honour.

For nature study, a Voyager reviews the story of Nicodemus and relates it to the life cycle of the butterfly or draws a life-cycle chart of the caterpillar giving the spiritual significance and completes a Nature honour not previously earned. The Voyager can plan a list of at least five nature related activities that may be used for Sabbath afternoons as part of advanced requirements.

For outdoor living, with a party of not less than four, including an experienced adult counsellor, the Voyager goes on a 25km hike in a rural wilderness area, including one night in the open or in tents. The expedition planning should be a joint effort of the party and all food needed should be carried. From notes taken, they participate in a group discussion led by their counsellor, on the terrain, flora and fauna, as observed on the hike. The Voyager can also complete one Recreational honour not previously earned and pass a test in Voyager first aid. To achieve advanced requirements in this field, they can design and build five articles of camp furniture and design an entrance for your club camp that could be used for a Camporee. In lifestyle enrichment, the aim is to complete one honour in Outreach Ministries, Health and Science, Household Arts, Outdoor Industry, or Vocational categories, not previously earned.

Guide

This class is for a teenager 15 years of age who is in Year 11/Grade 10 or its equivalent and is an active member of Pathfinder Club. They should know and understand the AY Legion of honour. They can select and read one book of their choice from the Teen Book Club list, plus a book on local church history (in their division or country). They can also complete the Stewardship honour as an advanced requirement.

For spiritual discovery, they discuss how the Christian can possess the gifts of the Spirit as described by Paul in his letter to the Galatians and study and discuss how the Old Testament Sanctuary Service points to the cross and the personal ministry of Jesus. They should hold a current memory gem certificate, read and outline 3 stories of Adventist pioneers and tell these stories during a Pathfinder Club, AY or Sabbath School Worship time and read Steps to Christ and write a one-page report/essay. As a group (or individually), they can undertake community outreach by helping organize and participate in one of the following, making a friendship visit with a shut-in person, adopting a person or family in need and assisting them or any other outreach of your choice approved by their leader. They should also participate in a discussion on witnessing to other teenagers and put some of the guidelines into practice in a real situation. To achieve an advanced requirement, they can either bring two friends to at least two meetings sponsored by their church or help plan and participate in at least four meetings of youth evangelism or similar events.

For friendship development, in group discussion and by personal inquiry, they should examine their attitudes to two of the following topics, choosing a career, moral behaviour, sex and dating, or choosing a life partner, and for advanced requirements, they can write (minimum of 750 words.) or give an oral presentation (minimum ten minutes) on the subject of "How to make and keep friends."

In health and fitness, they can make a presentation to elementary students on the subject of the laws of good health, and complete one of the following activities, writing a poem or article for possible submission to one of the Health/Temperance Journals of the church, individually or as a group, organize and participate in a "Fun Run" or similar activity as well as discussing and recording their physical training program in preparation for this event. Another achievement requirement is to read pages 102-125 in the book "Temperance" by Ellen White, and pass the true/false quiz, and complete the honour in Nutrition or lead a group through the Physical Fitness honour. In advanced requirements, they can seek God's plan regarding sexual behaviour – AIDS & STD's.

For organisation and leadership development, following discussion, they can prepare a flow chart on denominational organization, with special details for their division, attend a conference sponsored Basic Pathfinder Staff Training Course, and plan and teach at least two requirements of any Pathfinder honour for a group of Junior Pathfinders.

In Nature, a Guide will read the story of Jesus' childhood in the Desire of Ages chapter 7 and relate it to the place of Nature Study in His education and ministry by going orally before an audience on original nature lessons (parable) drawn from your study and observations. The Guide then completes either the Ecology or Environmental Conservation honour.

For outdoor living, Guides go on a two-night pack camp, involving the discussion of the equipment to be taken, plan and cook in a satisfactory manner a three-course meal on an open fire and complete an object of lashings or rope work and one Honour not previously earned which can count towards the Aquatic, Sportsman, Recreation, or Wilderness Master. For lifestyle enrichment, a Guide completes an honour in Outreach Ministries, Outdoor Industries, Vocational, Health and Science, or Household Arts not previously completed.

Guide represents the last of the Pathfinder progressive achievement classes. However, a stand-alone class, the Master Guide class, is available for those who wish to become Pathfinder leaders, having previously undergone the Teen Leadership Training (TLT) programme, allowing for full leadership development.

Pathfinder Honours

Pathfinder club honours are a vital component of the Pathfinder club experience. These honours are designed to help young people develop essential skills, explore new interests, and cultivate a sense of personal responsibility. The Pathfinder club honours cover a wide range of topics, including nature, crafts, vocations, and religious studies. Each honour has specific requirements that participants must fulfil, often involving tasks such as completing a project, learning new information, or demonstrating proficiency in a particular skill.

The Pathfinder honours were first introduced at a General Conference Youth Advisory in 1927, while the first handbook listing the honours requirements was published in 1928, initially sixteen such honours made the inaugural list. Ever since, there have been many honours introduced, some modified from previous versions. Some honours may be specific to a geographical area due to the nature of the subject under discussion, however, many of the honours have worldwide scope.

There are more than 500 Pathfinder honours available for completion in all the Pathfinder classes, in the following categories: Arts & Crafts, Health & Science, Household Arts, Nature, Outdoor Industries, Recreation, Vocational and Spiritual Growth, Outreach and Heritage (see Appendix C).

One of the key benefits of participating in Pathfinder club honours is the opportunity for young people to explore new interests and develop valuable skills. Through the pursuit of honours, Pathfinders have the chance to discover their passions and talents, and to develop new hobbies and interests. This can help them to build self-confidence and self-esteem, as well as providing a sense of accomplishment and pride in their abilities. Honours also encourage participants to develop a sense of personal responsibility, as they must take the initiative to complete the requirements and demonstrate their knowledge and skills. This can help young people to develop important life skills such as time management, organisation, and perseverance.

In addition to personal development, Pathfinder club honours also provide valuable opportunities for social interaction and teamwork. Many honours involve group projects or activities, which can help participants to develop their communication and collaboration skills, as well as fostering a sense of community and belonging within the club. By working together to complete honours, young people can form strong bonds with their peers and adult leaders and learn to appreciate the value of teamwork and cooperation.

Furthermore, many Pathfinder club honours are designed to instil values such as respect for nature, service to others, and a strong moral character. Through participation in honours focused on environmental conservation, community service, and ethical decision-making, young people can develop a strong sense of personal integrity and a commitment to making a positive impact on the world around them. These values are fundamental to the mission of the Pathfinder club, and honours play a crucial role in helping young people to internalise and live out these principles in their daily lives.

Pathfinder club honours also provide young people with valuable opportunities for personal growth, skill development, social interaction, and moral education. Through participation in honours, Pathfinders have the chance to explore new interests, develop important life skills, and cultivate a strong sense of personal responsibility and integrity. The pursuit of honours can be a rewarding and enriching experience for young people and can help to build a solid foundation for their future success and well-being.

There are several honours available for every Pathfinder class, usually in different categories. Every Pathfinder ought to be encouraged to take as many honours as possible to fully experience the rich breadth of knowledge and skills to enhance their development. By working with their club counsellors, parents and/or guardians, each Pathfinder can the select the honours appropriate for their level, from basic to advanced.

Submitting a new honour

So, how are new honours introduced? First, the current honours checklist is crosschecked to see if the proposed honour is not already in circulation, this aims to avoid duplicity. Once the check is completed, a request is made to the local Conference Pathfinder Director, who verifies that the proposed new honour meets the criteria. The proposed honour is then submitted to the Division Pathfinder Specialty Committee Chairperson, who passes it on to the Pathfinder Honour Study Committee for approval. If approved, the honour is submitted to the General Conference Honour Committee for final approval and processing. The Honour Committee Chairperson sends a letter of recognition and thanks to the author, with a copy to the local Conference Pathfinder Director. However, if not approved, the honour is returned to the author with a written explanation for reasons of rejection or a need for revision if required/requested.

Club Curriculum

The curricula for both the Adventurer and Pathfinder clubs are six-year programmes each, starting with the Little Lamb in pre-school to Helping Hand in Year 4, progressing as the child gets older, and building on pre-existing knowledge from the previous attainment level. The age-specific Adventurer curriculum is designed to meet the specific needs of the very young children aged 4 years to 9 years old, generating their interest in learning about themselves and their world while challenging them to enrich their experiences in living for Jesus Christ.

The Adventurer club aims to provide a holistic approach to child development with the club's curriculum offering them a range of exciting and educational activities that promote physical, mental, and spiritual growth. The Adventurer club curriculum is based on the development of six core areas: spiritual, mental, physical, emotional, social, and family. These areas form the foundation of the club's activities and are integrated into every aspect of the curriculum.

In the spiritual realm, children are introduced to basic biblical concepts and principles through age-appropriate lessons and activities. They learn about the love of God, the importance of prayer, and the significance of living a life of faith. The club also encourages children to develop a personal relationship with God and cultivate a deeper understanding of their faith. Class counsellors, parents and guardians are encouraged to model their spiritual lives to the young children, who by beholding can develop their own spiritual life.

The mental aspect of the curriculum focuses on nurturing intellectual curiosity and creativity. Children are encouraged to explore new ideas, solve problems, and think critically. They engage in activities that challenge their cognitive abilities and foster a love for learning. The best platform for the full mental development is through their interaction with their own peers.

Physical development is also a key component of the Adventurer club curriculum. Children are taught the importance of regular exercise, healthy eating habits, and personal hygiene. They engage in a variety of physical activities such as hiking, camping, and team sports, which help them develop strength, coordination, and endurance.

Emotional well-being is also emphasised in the curriculum. Children are taught how to recognise and manage their emotions, as well as how to empathise with others. They learn the value of self-control, resilience, and positive thinking.

The social aspect of the curriculum encourages children to build positive relationships with their peers and elders. They learn the importance of cooperation, teamwork, and good manners. The club also provides opportunities for children to participate in community service projects, teaching them the value of giving back and making a positive impact in their surroundings.

The family component of the curriculum emphasises the importance of strong family relationships. Children are encouraged to spend quality time with their families, communicate openly with their parents, and learn about the significance of family values. The family component is one that can easily be overlooked, so club leaders ought to be intentional about integrating the family into the Adventurer ministry. The Adventurer curriculum forms the foundation of the Pathfinder curriculum for the older children aged 10 years to 15 years old.

On the other hand, the Pathfinder curriculum is a standard curriculum divided into six age-specific classes, namely, Friend class for 10-year-olds to Guide class for 15-year-olds. The curriculum aims to meet the special needs of this particular age group and is self-contained, with requirements in the areas of spiritual, physical, history, nature and outdoor skills. Classes or individuals may also choose to complete extra requirements to achieve an advanced level. It is important to understand that completion of the curriculum at every level allows the child to progress to the next level with ease, building on previous knowledge.

The Pathfinder club aims to also provide a holistic approach to the development of young people by offering a balanced programme that promotes physical, mental, spiritual, and social development. The club's curriculum is an essential part of this programme and provides a framework for guiding young people towards becoming responsible and productive members of society.

The Pathfinder club curriculum is designed to be comprehensive and flexible, allowing for the inclusion of a wide range of activities and experiences. It is divided into six main areas: outdoor skills, health, fitness, nature, crafts, and vocational training. Each of these areas is further broken down into specific requirements and activities that club members can complete to earn various honours and awards.

The outdoor skills component of the curriculum focuses on teaching young people how to navigate and survive in the wilderness, as well as how to care for and respect the environment. This includes activities such as camping, hiking, and orienteering. The health and fitness component encourages club members to develop healthy habits and engage in regular physical activity. This includes learning about nutrition, participating in sports, and earning certifications in first aid and CPR.

The nature component of the curriculum is designed to help young people appreciate and understand the natural world. This involves learning about ecosystems, conservation, and wildlife. The crafts component encourages club members to develop creativity and manual dexterity through activities such as sewing, woodworking, and art. Finally, the vocational training component is aimed at helping young people explore potential career paths and develop work-related skills.

One of the strengths of the Pathfinder club curriculum is its adaptability. Club leaders have the freedom to tailor the programme to the specific needs and interests of their Pathfinders. This allows for a high level of engagement and motivation among club members, as they can pursue activities that they are passionate about. Additionally, the curriculum provides a framework for developing important life skills such as teamwork, leadership, and problem-solving.

Overall, the Pathfinder club curriculum is an essential tool for guiding young people towards becoming well-rounded individuals who can make a positive impact in the world. By providing a wide range of activities and experiences, the curriculum helps to nurture the physical, mental, spiritual, and social development of club members. It is a valuable resource for both club leaders and young people, and its impact can be felt in the personal growth and development of its members.

There are several ways of delivering the class work, but a combination of individual, small group or class teaching may be required to maximise each child's learning. Each teacher should understand the curriculum and plan the teaching accordingly, so that subject areas that link can be delivered in tandem.

Teaching Adventurers

Teaching Adventurers can be both a challenging and fulfilling experience. As teachers, it is important to create an environment that is both stimulating and nurturing, where young children can thrive and develop a love for learning. Here are some key strategies for teaching young children effectively.

First and foremost, it is important to create a safe and welcoming classroom environment. Young children thrive in an environment where they feel safe to explore, take risks, and make mistakes. This can be achieved by setting clear and consistent rules and routines, providing ample opportunities for free play and exploration, and building positive relationships with each student.

Another key aspect of teaching young children is to make learning fun and engaging. Young children learn best through hands-on, interactive experiences. Incorporating play-based activities, arts and crafts, music, and movement into the curriculum can help capture children's attention and keep them engaged in learning. It is also important to tap into children's natural curiosity and interests to make learning relevant and meaningful to them.

In addition, effective communication is essential when teaching young children. This involves using simple and clear language, providing visual aids and demonstrations, and using a variety of teaching methods to accommodate different learning styles. It is also important to actively listen to children, encourage questions, and provide opportunities for children to express themselves in a safe and supportive environment.

Furthermore, building a strong foundation in social and emotional skills is crucial when teaching young children. This involves teaching them how to regulate their emotions, solve problems, communicate effectively, and build positive relationships with their peers. It is important to create opportunities for children to work together, share, and resolve conflicts in a constructive manner.

Finally, it is important for teachers to collaborate with parents and guardians to support children's learning and development. This involves sharing information about children's progress, seeking input on children's interests and needs, and working together to create a consistent and supportive learning environment both at home and at school.

Teaching young children requires a delicate balance of nurturing, engaging, and challenging young minds. By creating a safe and welcoming environment, making learning fun and engaging, communicating effectively, building social and emotional skills, and collaborating with parents, teachers can help young children develop a love for learning that will last a lifetime.

Teaching Pathfinders

Teaching Pathfinders, who are mostly teenagers, can also be a challenging task, as they are at a stage in their lives where they are rapidly developing both academically and personally. As a teacher, it is important to understand the unique needs of teenagers in order to effectively engage and motivate them. As a teacher for Pathfinders, I explore some effective strategies for teaching teenagers that have served me well.

First and foremost, it is essential to establish a positive and supportive classroom environment. Teenagers thrive in an environment where they feel respected, valued, and safe. As such, teachers should strive to create a classroom atmosphere that encourages open communication and collaboration. Building strong relationships with students and showing genuine interest in their well-being can go a long way in creating a positive learning environment.

One of the most effective ways to teach teenagers is to make the material relevant and engaging. Teenagers are often more motivated to learn when they can see the real-world applications of what they are studying. Incorporating current events, pop culture, and practical examples into lessons can help make the material more relatable and interesting for teenagers.

Another important aspect of teaching teenagers is to provide them with opportunities for independence and autonomy. Teenagers are at a stage in their lives where they are eager to assert their independence and make their own decisions. By giving them opportunities to take ownership of their learning, such as through project-based learning or student-led discussions, teachers can help teenagers develop important critical thinking and problem-solving skills.

In addition to providing opportunities for independence, it is also important to set clear expectations and boundaries for teenagers. Setting high expectations and holding students accountable for their work can help instil a sense of responsibility and discipline. At the same time, it is important for teachers to be flexible and understanding of the unique challenges that teenagers face, such as peer pressure, social dynamics, and personal struggles.

It is also important to recognise that teenagers have diverse learning styles and preferences. Some students may excel in traditional classroom settings, while others may benefit from more hands-on or experiential learning opportunities. Being able to adapt and differentiate instruction to meet the needs of individual students is crucial for effective teaching.

Finally, teaching teenagers requires a nuanced and empathetic approach. By creating a positive and supportive classroom environment, making the material relevant and engaging, providing opportunities for independence, setting clear expectations and boundaries, and recognising diverse learning styles, teachers can effectively engage and motivate teenagers in their learning. As a teacher, it is essential to be understanding and patient with teenagers, recognising that they are navigating a complex and formative stage of their lives.

Club Activities

The Adventurer and Pathfinder clubs offer a wide range of activities for its members. These activities are designed to help young people develop valuable life skills, leadership abilities, and a strong sense of community. A variety of activities ranging from outdoor adventures to community service projects are on offer to cater to the diverse interests and abilities of the children.

One of the most popular and highly anticipated activities is camping. Camping trips provide young people with the opportunity to connect with nature, learn valuable outdoor skills, and build lasting friendships. These trips often include activities such as hiking, fishing, and outdoor cooking, which help club members develop important survival skills and self-reliance. Whether it's setting up tents, cooking over an open fire, or hiking through the wilderness, camping trips offer countless opportunities for young people to learn and grow.

In addition to camping trips, the clubs also offer a range of community service projects. These projects provide young people with the opportunity to give back to their communities and make a positive impact on the world around them. From volunteering at local charities to organising fundraising events, these activities help club members develop a strong sense of empathy and compassion.

However, it is worth to note that much of the curriculum is organised for the children in the pursuit of achievement of awards and honours. The Adventurer awards and Pathfinder honours both aim to help the young people develop a diverse range of skills, from outdoor survival to leadership and communication. By working towards these awards and honours, club members can challenge themselves to grow and develop their abilities in a supportive and encouraging environment.

Physical activities are also an important part of the clubs. Members participate in sports such as basketball, football, and swimming, as well as outdoor recreational activities like hiking, rock climbing, and biking. These activities not only promote physical fitness and health but also teach important life skills such as teamwork, discipline, and perseverance.

In addition to these activities, the clubs also focus on spiritual growth and development. Children often participate in religious services, prayer meetings, and Bible study groups, where they can explore their faith and learn about important values like love, forgiveness, and compassion. These activities are designed to help young people develop a strong moral compass and a sense of purpose in life. Recently, a popular way of engaging the young people has been through the Adventurer and Pathfinder Bible Experience (ABE & PBE) programmes. Each year, preselected books of the Bible are chosen as study texts from which Adventurers and Pathfinders are tested for their knowledge, with each team coming up against other teams, progressively from Local, Conference, Union up to Division level (Finals).

Family

The Adventurer and Pathfinder clubs focus on the holistic development of young people and provide an avenue for family involvement and bonding, as parents and siblings often participate in the clubs' events and activities. Many of the events and activities are designed to be family-friendly, encouraging parents and siblings to join in the fun. When the whole family is involved, there is a sense of community and promotion of togetherness.

The emphasis on family involvement creates an opportunity for families to spend quality time together, in an otherwise busy environment, and engage in shared experiences that can strengthen their bonds. Whether it's going on a camping trip together as is often the case with Adventurers, participating in community service projects, or attending meetings and ceremonies, families have the chance to connect and build meaningful memories together. Photographs and videos taken during such events cement the beautiful memories that are created.

In addition to promoting family togetherness, the clubs also create a supportive community for its members. Families are often encouraged to participate in club meetings, events, and service projects, fostering a sense of belonging and camaraderie among both Adventurers and Pathfinders and their families. This creates a positive and nurturing environment that can be especially beneficial for young people as they navigate the challenges of adolescence.

Furthermore, the clubs provide opportunities for families to connect with other like-minded individuals and families. Through group activities and events, families can form new friendships and support networks within the Adventurer and Pathfinder communities. This not only benefits the individual families but can also create a sense of extended family and support for all involved.

The emphasis on family-friendly activities and the creation of a supportive community allows the clubs to not only enrich the lives of its members but also strengthen family relationships. Whether it's a shared camping trip, a community service project, or an Adventurer or Pathfinder ceremony, families can connect, grow, and create lasting memories together within the framework of these clubs.

Church

What has the church got to do with the Adventurer and Pathfinder ministries? Shouldn't these ministries run separately to the church activities and programmes? Well, the Biblical concept of "Church" comes from the term "ekklēsia" which refers to a local congregation but can also comprehensively refer to the church as the totality of Christians everywhere.

Church is not the building where people gather for worship, but the people gathered. The people in question are the family members who make the church family when they come together to celebrate Jesus Christ and His teachings and be part of God's plan of redemption for humankind. This means the church does not exist for its own sake, but rather to accomplish the commission that was given to it by its Lord (Matthew 28:18-20).

The Adventist Youth Ministries programme of the Seventh-day Adventist Church (SDA) church comprises three broad categories, namely: Adventurers (ages 4-9 years old), Pathfinders (ages 10-15years old) and Youth (ages 16-30+ years old). This template, as prescribed in the SDA church manual, provides a rich pathway for any child in the church to belong to a particular ministry and undergo discipleship for Christ. This is why the church nominates leaders in both Adventurer and Pathfinder ministries to work closely for and with the young people. The involvement of the wider church community allows for the complete development of a strong youth ministry that includes spiritual, mental, and physical development of each individual youth.

The Adventurer and Pathfinder ministries, if you like, are the evangelism arms of the church, allowing for young people of any religious persuasion, or none, to be part of the programmes. The main goal of these ministries is for discipling young people for Christ.

As the church through its board sets operational budgets for each of the church departments, care and prudence should be observed to appropriate enough resources for the running of these ministries. The church board, the operational authority of the local church, should ensure these ministries are totally catered for their smooth running.

The Adventurer and Pathfinder clubs bear the responsibility of reporting back to the church board and the church on the ongoing outcomes from their ministries, such as number of Bible study contacts, baptisms and class investitures. As the church hears and sees the fruitage from these ministries, more young people will inevitably be encouraged to enrol and take part.

One of the fundamental learning outcomes is to help the young Pathfinders understand how the SDA church is organised, and the various roles of the Pastor, Elders and Departmental leaders. The Pathfinders are allowed to sit as observers at a Church Business Meeting to appreciate how the church conducts its business. Following their attendance, each Pathfinder is encouraged to make a summary of the proceedings and share these with his/her class, completing this as work done towards the investiture requirements.

School and Community

In communities around the world, Adventurer and Pathfinder clubs have become a beloved and integral part of many young people's lives. These ministries, which are now global and are operated by the SDA Church, aim to provide an inclusive and supportive environment for the youth to learn valuable life skills, develop a love for nature and outdoor activities, and grow in their personal spirituality.

One of the most remarkable aspects of the clubs is the sense of community that they foster. Members of the club form strong bonds with their peers and adult leaders, creating a support network that extends far beyond the regular club meetings and activities. These connections often last a lifetime, as former Pathfinders continue to stay in touch with each other and give back to the next generation of participants.

The sense of community within the Adventurer and Pathfinder clubs also extends to the wider community in which they operate. Adventurers and Pathfinders frequently engage in service projects, volunteering their time and energy to make a positive impact on their neighbourhoods and beyond. Whether it's cleaning up local parks, visiting elderly care facilities, or organising food drives for those in need, they are always looking for ways to give back and be a force for good in the world.

Furthermore, the Adventurer and Pathfinder clubs often collaborate with other community organisations such as schools and businesses, forging partnerships that benefit everyone involved. This not only helps to strengthen the clubs' presence in the community but also exposes its members to a wide range of experiences and opportunities that they might not have encountered.

The impact of Adventurer and Pathfinder clubs on the community is undeniable. By instilling values of service, leadership, and teamwork in its members, the clubs help to create a generation of young people who are compassionate, capable, and eager to make a difference in the world. The community, in turn, benefits from the positive influence of these young leaders and the projects and initiatives they undertake.

The Adventurer and Pathfinder clubs are vibrant and active contributors to the communities in which they operate, fostering a sense of unity, service, and leadership among its members and leaving a lasting impression on those around it. The values and skills that Adventurers and Pathfinders learn through their participation in the club not only benefit them as individuals but also enrich and strengthen the communities they are a part of.

The Adventurer and Pathfinder clubs and the school symbiotically play a crucial role in the development and growth of young children by providing a supportive and nurturing environment that helps them build essential skills and values that will serve them well throughout their lives.

The clubs provide a variety of activities such as camping, community service, and leadership training, all of which are designed to help young people build character, develop important life skills and ensuring the young people develop physically, mentally, and spiritually. The young people learn the importance of teamwork, communication, and responsibility, while also developing a strong sense of self-worth and confidence.

School, on the other hand, is an educational institution where young people gain knowledge and skills that will help them succeed in life. In addition to academic learning, schools also play a crucial role in teaching important social and emotional skills, such as empathy, communication, and problem-solving. The school environment provides opportunities for young people to interact with their peers, form friendships, and learn how to navigate social situations.

The Adventurer and Pathfinder clubs and the school serve as important pillars in the development of young individuals, providing a supportive and enriching environment that helps young people grow and flourish. Both institutions are essential in helping young people become well-rounded individuals who are prepared to face the challenges of the future and gain important skills and values that will serve them well throughout their lives.

Teen Leadership Training

One of the most important aspects of the Pathfinder programme is to develop passionate leaders of tomorrow. The Pathfinder ministry was born out of young people leading others and so the essence of training our teen Pathfinders to become leaders of tomorrow will ensure that the ministry has a certain future. Pathfinders who have gone through the rigours of the programme, when trained as leaders, will empower other young people to enrol in the ministry.

The Teen Leadership Training (TLT) programme was designed to challenge and empower the teen Pathfinder with the necessary leadership skills to help them become future leaders who will make a difference. Of prime importance is the development of special leadership traits such as influencing others to think, act and follow. As a leader, you are called to direct, guide, influence the thoughts, feelings and behaviour of those you lead to a particular goal. This is best done through the example of Jesus Christ's leadership style - servant leadership - modelled on serving others first. Like Jesus, the TLT Pathfinder is called to set an example that others will choose to follow.

The TLT Pathfinder needs to have self-belief, courage, determination, dedication, and competitive drive. One of the fundamental tenets of the TLT programme is that the Pathfinder must be willing to sacrifice the little things in life for the things that matter, learning to give of themselves and how to receive from others. It is not only about getting to be known but getting to know others as well. Creativity is a non-negotiable trait, as young people are easily bored of doing the same old thing. So, using the vast array of resources available, a creative TLT member will always strive to enhance the experience that Pathfinder ministry affords. The energy, commitment and enthusiasm that teens have can be better channelled to find newer ways of delivering the programme, providing strength to live this life while preparing for the greater life as children of God.

So, who can enrol for the TLT programme? The TLT programme is optional, available to those who wish to advance into leadership positions. It is possible that not all teen Pathfinders may choose to take part. The TLT programme is part of, not separate from, the Pathfinder club so a TLT Pathfinder has first got to be a member of the Pathfinder club. However, a TLT Pathfinder should not be seen as superior or better than any regular Pathfinder, only that they are Pathfinders who have volunteered to help lead others. Prospective TLT members need to know in advance that it is a 4-year programme, progressively training in leadership, therefore, a strong commitment over that training period is required from the start.

The TLT programme can be run locally by the Pathfinder club, with the Club Director or TLT mentors overseeing the training or as a Conference-led programme, allowing for TLT members to gain useful experience among peers from different clubs in the local Conference.

A Pathfinder wishing to join the TLT Programme is required to complete a TLT application form and obtain three recommendations. Each club or Conference will establish its own TLT Council, which assesses the TLTs commitment to Pathfindering, their appropriate maturity level, and Christian witness, which will formulate the recommendations. At this point, the TLT Council will work with the Pathfinder to select an appropriate TLT mentor, who together with the club Director, will sign the application as a commitment to the TLT and his/her success. Following enrolment into the TLT programme, a new TLT must complete a minimum 60-day probationary period, during which period the club administration will evaluate the TLTs commitment to the programme, with a recommendation for successful completion of the probation or dismissal from the programme. Regular reviews are made to assess the TLT Pathfinder's progress. If there is any unbecoming conduct or failure to complete assignments, a review of the TLT Pathfinder will occur, with possible disciplinary action taken, up to and including dismissal from the TLT programme. These measures may appear draconian, however, being a TLT requires great responsibility.

The TLT programme is organised in four levels, from entry level 1 to level 4, each level taking approximately a year to complete. At each level, the TLT Pathfinder is devoted to also work towards the age or grade-appropriate Pathfinder achievement class. Level 1 TLT works towards the Voyager requirements and fulfils the administrative and outreach operations, level 2 TLT works towards the Guide requirements and fulfils the teaching and activities operations, level 3 TLT works towards the Basic Staff Training and Master Guide requirements and fulfils the records and special operations, and level 4 TLT works towards Master Guide new skills requirements and fulfils the counsellor and special operations. All TLTs, regardless of the level, are required to take the Club Orientation Programme (COP) review.

Master Guide

Master Guide, the highest level of leadership within the Adventurer/ Pathfinder programmes, is a special ministry devoted to the development and mentoring of youth leadership, focusing on Christ-like leadership to disciple others. The Master Guide vision is to see all young people saved through training for leadership and service to God and fellow human beings. The curriculum is intentional - training and equipping those who wish to take an active part in local youth ministry.

Pledge
"Loving the Lord Jesus, I promise to take an active part in Adventurers, Pathfinders and Youth Ministries, doing what I can to finish the work of the gospel in all the world".

Law
"The Master Guide Law calls me to be an example in Word, Conduct, Love, Spirit, Faith, and Purity." (Based on 1 Timothy 4:12)

Song
Press on forward Master Guides with holy boldness; we're invested with great strength.

To help all the youth who choose to be with Jesus, and they long to follow Him.

To the lost souls we are giving the great message that constrains within our hearts.

There's a crown awaiting each of us in heaven, with bright stars which Jesus has for us.

Press on forward Master Guides with holy boldness; we're invested with great strength.

With a glorious torch that's lifted up towards heaven, will bring light into this world.

Though we're threatened by a world that's filled with darkness, we'll go forward without fear.

In the light that keeps on shining from our Saviour, to help guide us as we walk the AY path.

Prerequisites

The prerequisites for enrolling into the Master Guide programme are: be a baptised member of the Seventh-day Adventist Church, have a written recommendation from the local church board stating that one is a member in regular standing, be at least 16 to start the Master Guide leadership course and at least 18 years of age at completion, should have completed Basic Staff Certification for Adventurer or Pathfinder Club or the Introduction to Youth Ministry Certification and been involved for a minimum of one year in one of either Adventurer Club, Pathfinder Club or Youth Ministries, or in all three.

Master Guide requirements

Master guide requirements fall broadly under the headings of spiritual, skills, child, leadership, and fitness lifestyle development.

Spiritual development

The spiritual development starts with reading or listening to the book Steps to Christ and providing a summary based on ones understanding of the message. Secondly, the Master Guide enrols for a year's Daily devotion such as the devotional or another year long Bible reading plan that covers the four Gospels and read the

Desire of Ages. Thirdly, a 28-day devotional journal is recorded summarising what one learned in the devotional time and how it has helped their faith to grow. At the same time, they are encouraged to complete a seven-week personal spiritual development curriculum centred on Steps to Discipleship. Fourthly, the Master Guide aims to earn either an Adventurer or Pathfinder Evangelism Award, which may also include Daniel and Revelation seminars. Lastly, as part of doctrinal instruction, the Master Guide prepares a two-paragraph personal reflection on each of the 28 Fundamental Beliefs of Seventh-day Adventists, this in turn helps each candidate have a better understanding of what we believe and as a result be able to share their faith with others in their ministry.

Skills development

This is a varied section, requiring attendance and completion of workshops (each over an hour in duration) in the following subject areas - how to be a Christian leader and leadership skills, vision, mission and motivation, communication theory, listening skills, practical communication practices, understanding teaching and learning styles, creativity and resource development, how to prepare creative effective worships, principles of youth and children's evangelism, how to lead a child to Christ and understanding your Spiritual gifts.

Other specific workshops include risk management that focuses on Adventurer, Pathfinder and Youth activities, child abuse prevention, camping skills levels I to IV, knot tying and basic drill and marching.

Master Guides are encouraged to earn an honour not previously earned, at level 2 or 3, for example crisis intervention, nutrition or flags and hold a Current First Aid & CPR Certificate or its equivalent, supervise Adventurer and Pathfinder investiture achievement service or teach a Youth Sabbath School class for a year.

Child development

The Master Guide is required to attend a workshop dealing with child development, observe for a period of two hours a group of Adventurers, Pathfinders or AY or Youth, reflecting on their interactions and read or listen to the book Education by E. G. White and either Child Guidance or Messages to Young People.

Leadership development

The Master Guide is required to read or listen to a current book about Leadership Skills Development, for example, Ellen White on Leadership by Cindy Tutch, A Positive Church in a Negative World by Jonas Arrias, Take the Risk by Ben Carson or Help! I am being Followed by Clinton Valley. They also are required to conduct three creative worships for children and/or teenagers, assist in planning and leading a field trip for a group of Adventurers, Pathfinders or Sabbath School class, and teach at least two or three Pathfinder honours or Adventurer awards.

Fitness Lifestyle Development

In consultation with their doctor, a Master Guide embarks on a tailored personal physical fitness plan for three months and in a one-page essay describe what they learned during these physical fitness activities and the changes they are willing to make to "Care for the Body".

Adventurer and Pathfinder Bible Experience

One great way of encouraging children to come to Jesus is through the study of God's Word. The Word becomes a compass directing their paths. When every child immerses themselves in God's Word, they will learn to live for Jesus in this world. Jesus said, "Let the little children come to Me, and do not forbid them; for of such is the kingdom of heaven." Matthew 19:14. Jesus invites all children to come to Him, for of such is the kingdom of heaven. We should forbid none of His precious children from coming to Him.

The Adventurer (ABE) and Pathfinder Bible (PBE) Experience promotes and encourages in-depth Bible study and memorisation by both Adventurers and Pathfinders, enriching their understanding of scripture and growing their relationship with Christ. ABE and PBE provide a wonderful starting point for Bible study and a life-changing relationship with Jesus Christ. It is not all about memorisation but life application so that Adventurers and Pathfinders use what they study and apply it to their daily experience at home, school and church.

ABE and PBE are team-based challenges that test the group's knowledge of sections of scripture. Each year, a new section of scripture is assigned for study and subsequent testing, alternating between old and new testaments sections. After months of study, Adventurers and Pathfinders gather with other teams in their area to test their knowledge, with teams gaining first position advancing to the next stages of the experience, from Area to Conference, Union and finally the Division. The Division level forms the finals, typically held in April each year, for PBE it is held under the North America Division, whereas the Trans European Division holds both the ABE and PBE finals. As teams prepare, they meet together for study and revision, growing a bond that underpins every work they do. There is also the added sense of excitement that spurs participants on to higher levels of recall. It is a great programme that allows all to advance, based solely on their efforts. For some, the travel experience is often the pinnacle of their experience.

Teams are made up of a minimum of two to six members from a single club, with some clubs registering multiple teams based on the numbers interested. Each team is composed of six enrolled members, with one nominated as a team captain and another as a scribe. A club staff member, Pastor, or committed parent acts as the team's coach. Their role is to coordinate training and to motivate the team. Additional adults are welcome to assist with training, but there should be one official coach per club in charge of coordinating the team efforts of the club.

All team members must be in full dress uniform to participate at any level event. This uniform normally includes dress uniform shirt with proper insignia, dress uniform pants or skirt, authorised socks or stockings, authorised shoes, belt, scarf with slide, and Sash (see appendix D, E and F for Class A uniform).

I have found this part of the curriculum a very rewarding one, from personal experience as a parent of three young children and also as a local Adventurer and Pathfinder club Director. I have seen children take part in this programme from being novices to the level where they develop a love for the scriptures that so often belie their age. Genuine interest based on the aspiration of a deeper study and understanding of God's Word allows club leaders to nurture the young people in their amazing Bible journey.

ABE and PBE are exceptional programmes that prepare young people for a lifetime of faith and service by encouraging young people to delve into the Word of God and deepen their understanding of the Bible. The programme provides a platform for young individuals to not only study the scriptures but also apply them in their daily lives.

The first PBE event which took place in 2001 proved an instant hit, as Pathfinders eagerly participated in the rigorous study and memorisation of scripture verses, preparing for the annual PBE competition. The popularity of the PBE programme continued to grow over the years, with the programme expanding to include different levels of competition, from Area to Conference, Union, and ultimately, the Division level. Similarly, the ABE, a brand-new concept which was launched at the British Union Adventurer Camporee in 2018, was modelled on the PBE with a truncated version of the same study passages. ABE and PBE have now firmly become diarised in the annual calendar of events, with thousands of young people participating each year. The programme has evolved to include study guides, resources, and support for club leaders to help their Adventurers and Pathfinders succeed in the competition. Both programmes have continued to adapt to the digital age, with the introduction of online quizzes and study materials to make the process more accessible to all.

The impact of ABE and PBE on the participants has been profound. Through the programme, countless young people have developed a love for the scriptures and a deeper understanding of their faith. Furthermore, ABE and PBE promote teamwork and camaraderie among its participants. As young individuals work together to study and understand the Bible, they learn to appreciate the diversity of perspectives and interpretations. This fosters a sense of unity and mutual respect, while also encouraging healthy debate and discussion. These are important skills that will serve them well in their future endeavours, both in their personal and professional lives.

Additionally, ABE and PBE provides a platform for young people to harness their reading, writing and comprehension language skills that go beyond the study of God's Word into the school curriculum. Another great thing about ABE and PBE is that it brings people together, creating a sense of community and shared purpose. It's a chance to make new friends, work together, and grow in faith as a team.

My Memoirs

I traced the first footsteps of Doncaster Doves Bible Adventurers which started as a new Bible Experience team and reached the summit in the year 2022. Doncaster town had just recently undergone significant regeneration to attract businesses and investment into this historic part of South Yorkshire, United Kingdom. This renewal culminated in Doncaster submitting a bid to become a city during the platinum jubilee year of the reign of Her Majesty Queen Elizabeth II. If one could pick the ideal location for a town, Doncaster would be at the top of the list. The town is situated at the heart of the motorway network, with easy access to and from the M18, M1, A1(M), M62 and the M180, making 87% of the UK population reachable in only four hours' drive time. The flagship East Coast Main Line links the town by rail to the whole of the UK and on into Europe. Trains from Doncaster to London are fast and frequent, the journey takes around 88 minutes, with an average of 60 trains a day. The aforementioned made Doncaster town an exceptional place for business due to a perfectly connected rail, road, air and sea network. Doncaster grew from its strong industrial heritage to become a leader in the rail industry, a central hub for logistics such as Amazon and home to global brands in the manufacturing sector.

It was no wonder that the local club basked in Doncaster town's regeneration. Here, in not so well-known Bentley, a little corner of North Doncaster, six very young Adventurers from Doncaster SDA Church took on the mammoth challenge to become the first team ever from the church to participate in the Adventurer Bible Experience (ABE). The journey began in November 2021 when the club formed the inaugural ABE team, dedicated to studying the book of Ruth and 1 Kings chapters 1 to 6. The young Adventurers immersed themselves in the study of God's Word, registering further first place successes at the Conference and Union levels of testing and reaching the Trans-European Division (TED) finals summit in Belfast in April 2022.

The team's ascent to the summit of the ABE finals brought to memory the seismic conquest of Mount Everest, when Edmund Hillary and Sherpa Tenzing Norgay reached the 29,035-foot summit of Everest on 29 May 1953, becoming the first people to stand atop the world's highest mountain. Like the 1953 British expedition, which was oddly bottom-heavy with 350 porters, 20 Sherpas, and tons of supplies to support a vanguard of only ten climbers, the Bible Adventurers team was also supported by the church and the local Pathfinder and Adventurer clubs. The six Bible Adventurers in Doncaster were chosen as potential finalists, but, as they discovered, their amazing journey was only made possible by God, the Author of the book they were studying. Since then, Doncaster Doves Bible Adventurers have never looked back, enrolling new team members and entering subsequent ABE testing.

The ABE was established as an offshoot of the North American Division's PBE to cater for the younger age group. It is now such a runaway success with all the clubs such that the ABE is now firmly cemented in the Pathfinder Calendar. The concept is much like the PBE with adjustments that allow younger participants to take part.

Camporee

Camporees are the highlight in the calendar of Adventurer and Pathfinder events, with young people gathering for camping and outdoor activities with a common goal of building courage, confidence, character and leadership. There is a minimum number of days for a camporee to be useful, in some cases, especially the younger Adventurer children, a 3-day weekend camporee may be appropriate whereas for the older Pathfinder children, a week-long camporee is the usual choice.

Camporees require meticulous organisation and planning, from identifying a suitable outdoor location with the required facilities, a theme under which all the events take place, and a dedicated camporee committee that promotees the camporee to all clubs to encourage their attendance. Good camporee planning committees always plan to include new camping skills that can be learned by attendants, including new honours or awards that the young people can earn while camping, all geared towards the provision of opportunities for young people to gather, challenge themselves and gain or improve their outdoor skills. A theme provides guidance when choosing the activities and programme ideas.

It is important to plan well in advance to avoid disappointment in securing a reservation at the outdoor facility that will host the camporee, as these venues usually run out of dates very quickly. The best practice is to make sure the venues are booked years in advance, as long as the dates are also known in advance. A deposit may be required to secure a venue booking. Similarly, a very motivating camporee speaker will require advance booking to secure their ministry.

A camporee can both be held locally for local clubs within a Conference or be held in large territories such as Divisions. The latter, larger camporees, often end up becoming international camporees, allowing young people from across the globe to attend. The primary advantage of hosting an international camporee is the shared learning that comes from the groups from different parts of the world. It is at such times that cultures come together to learn from each other.

Costs for attending camporees vary, depending on the location of the camporee, with local camporees proving cost-effective than international camporees. The major cost drivers for international camporees include transport for the attendees and their camping equipment, visa and insurance requirements. However, it is possible to spread the cost for such camporees over a few years as long as it is planned in advance.

Parents of Adventurer are best to attend camporees with their children, allowing clubs to camp as a group of families to alleviate the need for staffing provision to meet the requirements for safe camping. However, Pathfinder clubs, with older children, do not need parents to accompany them as the club counsellors and staff will supervise them. A camporee provides an exciting and transformative event within the Adventurer and Pathfinder calendars, designed to provide a unique and memorable experience for young people.

The greatest emphasis for a camporee is the spiritual enrichment for the young people with daily worship services held in a large tent/marquee, inspirational talks on topics dear to the hearts of the young people, and prayer and reflection times. These are integral to the spiritual experience that helps the young people grow in their faith.

Camporees are not only about spiritual activities, but young people also get the chance to gain the full outdoor camping experience, including outdoor adventures such as hiking, orienteering, archery and other team building outdoor physical challenges. Camporees provide a platform for young people to earn awards and honours, encouraging them to develop new skills and expand their knowledge base.

Camporees also foster lifelong friendships and connections as young people from different backgrounds and regions come together, strengthening their bonds and learning about and appreciating the cultural diversity within their community.

Camporees typically conclude with a grand parade, where clubs display their flags and uniforms. The closing ceremony often includes a formal acknowledgment of achievements, awards, and a spiritual farewell.

While a camporee is many things to many people, the key component of any camporee is to offer a rich wholesome experience of outdoor activities that provide fun, enhance health but also attest to the spiritual development of the young people. For some, camping fun means to sit around the campfire with the smoke from the fires providing a backdrop to their conversations. Others cherish the sounds of the rain on tents at night. The main 'to do tasks' for organising a camporee are listed below.

Camporee Organisers

1. Choose a speaker, date and location (venue) of camporee
2. Secure the location (venue) with a deposit
3. Select camporee Chairperson and choose a camporee planning committee
4. Prepare an operational budget and determine camporee fees
5. Start promotion for club attendance - this will continue until the closing date of applications

6. Plan the full camporee programme and order patches, pins, certificates and other sundries in time.
7. Plan for water, sanitation, fuel supply, insurance, and permits
8. Plan for policing, first aid and health and safety. Produce final programme
9. Arrange for delivery of equipment and materials to campsite.
10. Make follow up reports, insurance, and evaluations

Camporee Attendees

1. Complete camporee application form
2. Obtain visa for international camporees
3. Secure attendance by paying the fee
4. Identify Pathfinder club staff and Counsellors or parents and guardians of Adventurers
5. Identify safeguarding, first aid and food handling, health and safety personnel for the group
6. Obtain parental consent and medical and allergy information
7. Purchase tents, outdoor sleeping bags, cooking utensils and other outdoor equipment.
8. Plan and organise transportation of attendees and their equipment
9. Arrange for an advance party to take and erect camping equipment on site
10. Purchase food for the whole camporee

My Memoirs

I remember with great fondness my club's attendance at a joint South England Conference (SEC) Adventurer and Pathfinder Camporee held during the Covid-19 pandemic at Phasels Wood Activity Centre in Hertfordshire, from 22 to 31 July 2022. We praised God that during the lockdown years when no outdoor events were possible our young people were able to use the online platforms to hold virtual camporees. This camporee was an inclusive camporee, not only limited to SEC clubs, with the attendance of a strong 51-man contingent from the Scottish Mission and seven Doncaster Doves Pathfinders, from the North England Conference.

The theme for that year's camporee 'God's World, Our World' emphasised that our loving God created this world for us to live in it and care for it and ultimately appreciate His love. The Holy Spirit guided the SEC Pathfinder Department in their planning for this camporee from the choice of the main speakers, the theme and activities and honours which were carefully chosen to reflect aspects of creation.

The main speakers for both camporees gave inspiring messages pointing the campers to Jesus, the ultimate Pathfinder. The first to arrive at the campsite were Adventurers for their camporee, held over the weekend, from Friday to Monday. The main speakers anchoring the programme for the Adventurers were Judy Clements OBE, SEC Children's Ministries Director and Craige Young, Director of BrixKidz. Judy's passion to lead children to a life-long commitment to Jesus Christ was evident in her messages to the Adventurers. Both Judy and Craige worked together to deliver inspiring messages to the Adventurers, the latter using real-life examples from the world of science to deliver spiritual object lessons.

As soon as the Adventurers had left the campsite, Pathfinders arrived the following day. Guest speaker, Pastor Eugene Carolus, from Cape Town, South Africa added an international flavour to the camporee. In his first message, Pastor Eugene pointed out that our Creator God wants to restore the intimate relationship fully enjoyed by Adam and Eve in the Garden of Eden. God created man in His own image and breathed the breath of life into Adam's nostrils, thus getting intimately into Adam's personal space. Eve, whom God created out of a rib taken out of Adam while he was in deep sleep, first saw God before being introduced to Adam. Our first parents' first sight was of their Creator God before everything else. He challenged the young people to make God first in their lives.

In his official address to Adventurers and Pathfinders, SEC Pathfinder Director, Pastor Clifford Herman welcomed the campers to the first SEC Camporee after 5 years, encouraging them to make new friends, build lasting memories and strengthen their relationship with Jesus, our best friend. He added "This is God's world, created for us to appreciate and love Him. It is also our world, given to us as stewards to live in it, care for His creation and build long-lasting friendships."

This camporee also showed what our young people had missed over the past few years, as the appetite for outdoor group activities was quenched by the array of activities on offer. Clubs were requested to book each attendee's activities online prior to camp, emphasising the 'green' nature of this camporee. The Adventurers were also treated to a special new award called Earth Keepers award. This new award was created by Vernon Noel, SEC Pathfinder Coordinator. Adventurers went out on a nature walk to appreciate all of God's nature and help them identify God's creation. Using cut out plastic bottles, they built a one-storey hotel using strings and cut out pieces of bamboo sticks admixed with collections of wood, leaves and grass.

On the nature walk, the Adventurers participated in a pollination count, naming flowers, and observing insects that landed on the flowers for a period of 10 to 15 minutes.

The camporee allowed each club to showcase the diversity of its members in terms of their nationalities, with clubs participating in a colourful parade in national dress and national flags. The parade added value to the message that all are welcome in Christ. The Doncaster Doves appreciated the generosity and hospitality of the SEC in allowing other clubs from outside the SEC to come to camp with them that year.

Hiking and Expedition

Hiking forms one of the major physical requirements for Pathfinder classes from Friend to Guide. There are two hikes, 8km for the younger or 25km for the older Pathfinders. In my experience, the hikes provide a very unique opportunity for the whole Pathfinder club to get involved in a team exercise, which leads to bonding among the group. One of hike's greatest draws is that anyone can get involved, with no set minimum distance. Whoever organises a hike, needs to meticulously plan the hiking terrain to ensure the health and safety of all involved.

The good news is that there is no one way to hike, in fact hiking is so versatile that it can be changed to suit the needs of your particular group taking into consideration where you go, how far you go and what you do on the way. The latter part can be essential as you can choose fun activities to complement the hiking experience.

It is important to maintain the beauty of hiking by not rushing the exercise and varying what you do on the way. Hiking is more than just the destination; it is more about the journey getting there. No two hikes will be the same; sometimes you may get lost in the terrain, or tiredness might befall members of your hiking team requiring significant pause in the speed or the weather elements might surprise you on the way. One of the ways we have always maintained interest in our hiking exercises is to vary the added activities along the way, allowing participants to get involved in team challenges such as treasure hunt, map reading and navigation and exploring local landmarks along the way.

The leader of a hiking exercise will ensure at the planning stage that health and safety checks are attended to ensuring that a formal, written risk assessment is performed, an emergency procedure protocol is formalised to help hikers know what to do in an emergency and that the correct ratios of number of supervising adults or counsellors to children is met. These health and safety checks, together with a complete activity form are shared with the hikers, and their parents and carers. As with many of the group activities, pertinent medical information on each of the hikers is collated and brought along with a first aid box to be used in case of an emergency.

The most important thing is that hiking is not just a trek into the mountains or treacherous terrain but even countryside footpaths and forest track can be used to good effect. The Pathfinders can learn more about map reading and navigation skills, team work, and their own physical status and durability during the hike. There is a lot to be gained when hikes are organised as part of a larger group of Pathfinders from different clubs.

My Memoirs

Our local club participated in an area-wide hike organised by Pathfinder Area Coordinators (ACs) as a group event. The aim of this particular hike was to allow Pathfinders to go back to nature to discover the beauty of God's creation during a group hiking experience in Bolton Abbey Estate in North Yorkshire on Sunday, 22 May 2022. The Pathfinders were also aiming to complete some of their basic requirements for outdoor events, in the immediate aftermath of lockdown years at the time of the Covid-19 pandemic. In keeping with the true meaning of a Pathfinder – a person who goes ahead and discovers or shows others a path or way – and true to their nature, two of our Pathfinder Area Coordinators led the group of pathfinders on this Sunday morning which was beautiful in its spring splendour.

Word was sent out to the participants – a total of 32 hikers – instructing them to meet in the Devonshire Arms Hotel & Spa car park, a perfect base from which to explore the breath-taking countryside. There were no late comers for the start time, and so the group accessed the trail via public footpaths, bridleways, and minor roads. The route was deliberately circuitous to build the required mileage. The pedometer registered 11.9 km (7.4 miles) in just over 4 hours, to the tune of aching limbs and a half-day's calories burned.

Along the way, on our circular trail, we were greeted by major landmarks, the most imposing one being the Priory Church and Ruins of an Augustinian Priory in its beautiful riverside setting at the heart of Bolton Abbey Estate. Our next trail phase led us to the second major landmark, the stepping stones which are synonymous with Bolton Abbey. These stones were used to help workers to cross the River Wharfe safely. Today, the 60 stepping stones offer the visitor a fun and challenging experience. Our group attempted to cross the stepping stones but retreated and crossed by the adjacent bridge. We followed the path from the stepping stone bridge upstream through the woodland, where we passed three fallen trees, all laden with coins. It is still a wonder who pushed the coins into the tree and how they did it.

Our Pathfinders found that one of the best things about hiking, apart from the hiking itself, is meeting many lovely and like-minded people along the way. For a pleasant experience, there is a certain etiquette that all hikers must abide by – the unwritten rules. For example, hikers must only leave traces of their hiking boots, not litter. Hikers must stay in touch with their group to avoid getting lost. It is also understood that no noise is good noise, so some would prefer to listen to favourite playlists via headphones. Lastly, hikers must observe the hiking hierarchy – with bikers yielding to hikers and hikers to horses.

"It was a great learning opportunity for all, especially for the Pathfinders that came long. We had a great time learning about God in nature, interacting with other Pathfinders, and getting the full benefits of the physical exercise," commented one Club Director. One of our Club Counsellors, concurred, "The hiking experience was tiring and amazing at the same time. I had the opportunity to see and appreciate God's handiwork in nature. It was rewarding to spend time with fellow Pathfinders. The pain in my feet will fade away, but the memories will stay with me forever."

While we held a debrief in the car park, we witnessed a helicopter land on the helipad, bringing visitors for a Sunday lunch at the Devonshire Arms Hotel & Spa. We could have enjoyed a quick escape by helicopter on our way back! The day out at Bolton Abbey was full of fun for all.

Drill and Marching

Drill and marching, both traditional elements of military training, have been around for centuries and even though some may view these activities as outdated or unnecessary in modern times, they continue to be an important part of military training. These methods, adopted into the Adventurer and Pathfinder ministries, help young people work together as a team as they execute any duty they are called upon, leading to building timing, physical coordination, discipline, orderliness and confidence. As a result, young people who gain these skills, have high regard and respect for authority. There is no other activity that can replace what drill and marching does, as young people develop group spirit within a club with everyone working together and having a sense of importance and belonging. Drill and marching, when done in a fun way, offers so much for our young people, and can be used during the following occasions: the local club programmes and ceremonies, Conference programmes and public ceremonies or parades.

First and foremost, drill and marching help instil discipline and teamwork. Young people learn to follow precise movements and commands, aiding them as they work together as a unit and respond quickly to orders. At the same time, drill and marching also help improve physical fitness and coordination as the repetitive movements of drill help build muscle memory and improve overall physical conditioning. In addition, marching requires young people to maintain a steady pace and posture, which can improve balance, coordination, and cardiovascular fitness.

Furthermore, drill and marching serve to honour and uphold Adventurer and Pathfinder values. These activities have been a part of Pathfinding for a long time and are a way to connect young people to the long line of others who have served before them. The common drill and march commands are given in the section below.

Stationary drill

Attention

The command will be given as "Pathfinders, attenTION!" This is a position of readiness in expectation of a word of command, and exactness is paramount. In this position, heels are placed together and in line, feet turned out to a 30-degree angle, knees braced, body erect, shoulders level with arms hanging straight down and elbows close to the sides, wrists straight, hands closed but not clenched, thumbs straight and to the front. The head is held up with the eyes open and looking forward. Usually, the young people should not be held in the "attention" position for any longer than it is necessary for the next anticipated word command.

Stand at Ease

This command is given as "Pathfinders, stand at EASE." This position, which allows no relaxation, is intermediate between attention and stand easy, therefore can be maintained without strain for a longer time than attention. The "stand at ease" position keeps the right foot still and the right leg braced back, bends the left knee, carries the left foot sharply to the left so that the feet are 20-30 cm apart, heels still in line, and the feet at the same relative angle as in "attention". The arms are brought behind the back but kept straight and the back of the right hand is placed in the palm of the left hand, the fingers and hands straight and pointing toward the ground or floor.

Stand Easy

This command is given as "Pathfinders, stand EASY." In the "stand EASY" position, the body is generally relaxed (head, body and limbs) however, there should be no movement of the feet, or lowering of the hips and no talking. Adjusting clothing and equipment is allowed in this position. It is worth noting that the "stand EASY" position can only be given from a "stand at EASE" position, not from attention.

Right Turn

The command is given as "Pathfinders, right TURN." Here, with both knees kept straight, a 90-degrere turn to the right on the right heel and the ball of the left foot is made, raising the left heel and right toe but keeping the weight of the body on the right foot. This is completed by bending the left knee and bringing the left foot sharply to the right, adopting the "attention" position.

Left Turn

The command is given as "Pathfinders, Left TURN." Here, with both knees kept straight, a 90-degrere turn to the left on the left heel and the ball of the right foot is made, raising the right heel and left toe but keeping the weight of the body on the left foot. This is completed by bending the right knee and bringing the right foot sharply to the left, adopting the "attention" position.

About Turn

This command is given as "Pathfinders, about TURN." In this command, both knees are kept straight, and a 180-degree turn to the right is made on the right heel and the ball of the left toot, raising the left heel and the right toe but keeping the weight of the body on the right foot. This is completed by bending the left knee and bringing the left foot sharply to the right, adopting the "attention" position.

Right Incline

This command is given as "Pathfinders, right in-CLINE." Here, both knees are kept straight, and a 45-degree turn is made to the right on the right heel and the ball of the left foot raising the left heel and the right toe but keeping the weight of the body on the right foot. This is completed by bending the left knee and bringing the left foot sharply to the right, adopting the "attention" position.

Left Incline

This command is given as "Pathfinders, left in-CLINE." Here, both knees are kept straight, and a 45-degree turn is made to the left on the left heel and the ball of the right foot raising the right heel and the left toe but keeping the weight of the body on the left foot. This is completed by bending the right knee and bringing the right foot sharply to the left, adopting the "attention" position.

Paces Forward

This command is given as "Pathfinders, paces forward MARCH." This requires movement carried out in quick time, stepping with the left foot forward, with the arms held by the sides, each pace approximately 50 cm.

Paces Back

This command is given as "Pathfinders, paces backward MARCH." This requires movement carried out in quick time, stepping with the left foot backward, with the arms held by the sides, each pace approximately 50 cm.

Drill on the March

Here, Marching plays its part in Drill. The group marches with precision with stepping of pace that is equivalent to that taken by the smallest member on parade. The marching starts from the potion of attention, however, if they are standing at ease when the "QUICK MARCH" command is given, they should first come to attention before stepping off, always stepping off with the left foot leading.

The following words of commands are always given on the LEFT foot: Quick MARCH, Slow MARCH, or Double TIME, Mark TIME (when marching), For-WARD, Change STEP, Eyes RIGHT, eyes FRONT, Change to quick TIME, Slow time, or Double TIME, About TURN and Left TURN. The only word of command given on the RIGHT foot is the Right TURN.

Quick MARCH
The command is given as "Pathfinders, quick MARCH." Here, they step off with the left foot while swinging the right arm forward and the left arm to the back and march straight in front. When marching, the heel must strike to the ground first with the weight coming forward over the ball of the foot as the moving leg passes the standing leg, and every pace, including the first, measures 60cm. The legs are swung forward naturally in a straight line, the arms are swung freely and straight from front to rear reaching the extreme end of their swing each time the heel touches the ground.

Halt
This command is given as "Pathfinders, HALT." Since this command is always given on the left foot, one further pace with the right foot is taken before a check pace of 60cm with the left foot by striking the left heel to the ground. The command is completed by bringing the right foot sharply to the left foot and snapping the arms to the sides and adopting the position of "attention".

Marking Time from the Halt

This command is given as "Pathfinders, mark TIME." Here, you only move the legs with the arms at the side and the whole upper body retains the position of "attention". The left foot is brought forward and up to commence marking time, raising the left knee and keeping the upper part of the leg at 45 degrees to the ground with the foot at a natural angle. Subsequently the knee is lowered, the toe is placed on the ground before the heel. The mark time will continue until the command "forward" or "halt" is ordered.

Changing Step when Marking Time

This command is given as "Pathfinders, change STEP." Since this command is given when the right foot is on the ground: take two successive mark time paces with the left foot; and continue marking time.

Halting from Marking Time

This command is given as "Pathfinders, HALT." As this command is given when the left knee is being raised, the movement of the left foot is completed and then halted by making a further beat with the right foot.

Mark Time on the March

This command is given as "Pathfinders, mark TIME." As this command is given on the left foot, complete a 60 cm pace with the right foot and commence to mark time on the next beat of the left foot, cutting the arms to the sides as the left knee is being raised.

Changing Step on the March

This command is given as "Pathfinders, change STEP." This command, in slow time, is given as the right foot is forward and on the ground, therefore complete the full pace with the left foot, then bring the right foot forward in quick time and place the instep of the right foot against the heel of the left foot before stepping off in slow time with the left foot. If this command is given in quick time, it is given as the right foot is forward and the ground, then complete a full pace with the left foot, bring the right foot forward in double time and place the instep of the right foot against the heel of the left foot, bringing the arms to the sides before stepping off in quick time with the left foot.

Moving Forward from Marking Time

This command is given as "Pathfinders, for-WARD." As this command is given as the left knee is being raised, complete the beat with the left foot and then make a further beat with the right foot and then as the right foot comes to the ground move the left foot and right arm forward and the left arm to the rear and proceed in quick time.

Left Turn in Quick Time

This command is given as "Pathfinders, turning on the march, left TURN." As this command is given on the left foot, bring the right knee forward and upward and remain balanced on the left leg, turn the right foot across the body while the the upper part of the leg horizontal (the right foot hanging in natural angle right knee in front of the left knee) which will bring the right foot directly above the ground in front of the left toe. Then vigorously straighten the right knee and drive the right foot to the ground, with the instep just ahead of the left toecap. As the right foot strikes the ground then move the left foot out in a new direction and continue with marching.

Right Turn on Quick Time

This command is given as "Pathfinders, turning on the march, right TURN." This is the only word command given on the right foot, so bring the left knee forward and upward and remain balanced on the right leg, turn the left foot across the body while the the upper part of the leg horizontal (the left foot hanging in natural angle and the left knee in front of the right knee) which will bring the left foot directly above the ground in front of the right toe. Then vigorously straighten the left knee and drive the left foot to the ground, with the instep just ahead of the right toecap. As the left foot strikes the ground then move the right foot out in a new direction and continue with marching.

About Turn in Quick Time

This command is given as "Pathfinders, about TURN." As this command is given as the left foot reaches the ground, take another pace with the right foot and cut the arms to the side at the same time, raise the left foot and turn body through 90 degrees to the right and place the left foot down with the instep in front of the toe on the right foot, then raise the right foot and turn the body through the further 90 degrees and place the right foot down, toe pointing in the new direction. Then raise the left foot and place it alongside the right foot and commence to swing the arms as the right foot leads off in the new direction.

Wheeling to the Right

This command is given as "Pathfinders, change direction right, right WHEEL." This command may be given on the right foot. When marching in columns, at this command, wheel on the circumference of a circle with a radius of 60 cm and will change direction through 90 degrees. The spread of the wheel is governed by the ability of those on the outside to keep pace by stepping out. The ones on the inner flank will glance outwards from the corner of their eyes and vary their pace accordingly, files in rear marching straight to their front and follow on the ground covered by the leading files.

Wheeling to the Left
This command is given as "Pathfinders, change direction left, left WHEEL." and the movements are the opposite of the wheeling to the right.

Doubling
This command is given as "Pathfinder, double MARCH." At this command, step off with the left foot and run on the balls of the feet with easy swinging strides, inclining the body slightly forward, but maintaining correct carriage. The following must be maintained - the feet must be picked up cleanly from the ground at each pace, and the thigh, knee and ankle joints must all work freely, the heels should not be raised toward the seat, but the foot carried straight to the front and the ball of the foot placed lightly on the ground, and the arms should be swung as in quick time except that they should be bent so that the forearm forms an angle of about 135 degrees with the upper arm.

Halting from Marching in Double Time
This command is given as "Pathfinders, HALT." As the command is given on the left foot, take a further check pace with the right foot and then the left foot and bring the right foot sharply to the left foot and the arms to the side.

Slow March
This command is given as "Pathfinders, slow MARCH." All slow MARCH commands are ordered when at the position of "attention", with the body erect and the arms steady at the sides, step off smoothly with the left foot, straightening the left knee with the toe raised 5cm from the ground and pointing downward. Then raise the right heel off the ground and, with a gliding motion, complete one pace, the forward part of the left foot coming to the ground. Lastly, bring each foot forward, straight to the front, pointing the toe forward and downward.

Sizing a club

It is important to correctly size the club according to height size to enable the Adventurers and Pathfinders know in which order to fall in. The sizing can be done either as a mixed boys and girls club (starting start with either the tallest boy or girl) or sizing the boys and girls separately, in similar fashion. The club will preselect markers (tallest boy or girl) who will be the first to fall in. If the tallest boy is preselected in a mixed parade, at fall in, they will be followed progressively by the shorter boys up to the shortest, then the shortest girls, up to the tallest girls. Counsellors fall in at the rear of the column, ladies first then men, after sizing is completed. However, if not mixed, then the tallest falls in, followed by the shortest of that gender.

Marker fall in

The first command is given as "Marker, fall IN". The designated marker (tallest) will come to "attention", march onto the parade ground and halt at a designated spot facing the Director and the marker will remain standing at "attention".

Tallest on the right, shortest on the left, boys front, girls rear, rank size

The second command is given as "Tallest on the right, shortest on the left, boys front, girls rear, rank SIZE". Here, Pathfinders or Adventurers will come to "attention" and march onto the parade ground with the girl marker falling in one pace behind the boy marker. The Pathfinders will form up on the left of the markers and arrange themselves according to size, supervised by the Director. The club remains standing at "attention".

From the right, by ranks, tell off
The third command is given as "From the right, by ranks, TELL OFF". The boy marker will call "front", the Pathfinder on his left "centre", the next Pathfinder "rear", and so on down the front rank from right to left. The girl Pathfinder on the far left of the rear rank will tell off without breaking the sequence, and so on from left to right, ending at the tallest girl marker.

Front rank right turn, rear rank left turn, right and left turn
The fourth command is given as "Front rank right turn, rear rank left turn, right and left TURN". The ranks turn in the nominated direction.

Form three ranks, quick MARCH!
The fifth command is given as "Form three ranks, quick MARCH." The Marker marches forward three paces and halts. The rear rank wheels to the right and follows the front rank. Under the direction of the Director, each Pathfinder moves into the centre, rear or front rank upon arrival in position. Each file, when completed, will turn to the front and remain at "attention". Adjustments to the left flank, in the creation of blank files, will be made during dressing.

Tallest on the right, shortest on the left, in single rank SIZE
The Pathfinders will come to attention, march onto the parade ground and form up on the left of the marker and arrange themselves according to size, supervised by the Director. When in position they will stand at "attention".

Pathfinders, NUMBER
The Pathfinders number from right to left. The Director will make sure that the Pathfinders know their number.

Odd numbers one pace forward, even numbers one pace backward, MARCH

The Pathfinders will take a pace forward or to the rear, in accordance with their numbers.

From the right, by ranks tell off

The marker will call "front". The Pathfinder on the left will call "centre", the next Pathfinder "rear", and so on down the front rank from right to left. The Pathfinder on the far left of the rear rank will tell off without breaking the sequence, and so on from left to right.

Front rank right turn, rear rank left turn, right and left turn

The ranks turn in the nominated directions.

Form three ranks, quick MARCH!

The rear rank wheels to the right and follows the front rank. Under the direction of the Director, each Pathfinder moves into the centre, rear or front rank and upon arrival in position halts. Adjustments to the left flank, in the creation of blank files, will be made during dressing.

Special Events

The annual calendar for Adventurer and Pathfinder clubs has special days that aim to bring these clubs into prominence within the local church and in the community. These special days, when carefully and intentionally planned, offer the children and their leaders an opportunity to exhibit everything that the clubs do, in so doing, raising awareness of these ministries.

Club induction and investiture

Induction and Investiture are grand occasions in the calendar of the Adventurers and Pathfinders programme, where young people are enrolled into the programme and after a year of instruction and study their achievements are duly celebrated. It should be the highlight of the calendar of events for the clubs. It is hugely important that the services are conducted and delivered in a dignified manner. The club Director should check with the local church Pastor at the beginning of the curriculum year to ring fence one Sabbath later in the year planned for the investiture to take place. It is best to have this date in place so that it can be announced at the time of the club induction to give Adventurers and Pathfinders a focus as they do their class work. The investiture can be held either during the Sabbath morning or the afternoon. The former offers the advantage of maximising the involvement of the whole church during the morning divine service. The club Director, in liaison with the local Pastor, also identifies a preacher for the day. The rest of the planning involves the club committee and the relevant Conference.

My Memoirs

In my own experience, I extended the invitation to our local Civic Mayor, local member of Parliament and local Government Councillors, to be part of the induction and investiture ceremonies, helping create a collaboration with community leaders that we serve. They all accepted the invitations and were part of the ceremonies. My advice is to plan these invitations early to avoid non-attendance as most of these dignitaries have other engagements which may cause a conflict. As guests of honour, they can address the club during the presentation and also give out the awards. A get together after these ceremonies gives the chance for the Adventurers and Pathfinders to build relationships. One such example is an investiture awards dinner that we hosted.

World Adventurer Day

Once a year, Adventurers celebrate a World Adventurer Day, which is typically held in the third Sabbath of May. All world Adventurer clubs are invited to participate together, using the outstanding resources created by the General Conference of Seventh-day Adventists Youth Department and additional resources offered by various world Divisions. Clubs are advised to utilise this day wisely, some in their local church, others come together with different clubs to meet as a large unit. The former allows the Adventurer club to get to know their church members, some of whom may already have children in the club. The parents who do not have children registered in the club can then develop interest for their children as the presentations are made to the church. It is best to extend an intentional invitation on this special day to would-be, prospective Adventurers who are not yet registered. At the same time, an open invitation to the community within the catchment area of the local church allows non-Adventist to enrol into the club. On the other hand, a club may attend a larger gathering of other clubs on the World Adventurer Day which has been organised by the local Conference, with the Adventurers afforded the opportunity of meeting up with like-minded Adventurers, learning from each other and creating lifelong friendships.

World Pathfinder Day

World Pathfinder Day is a special Sabbath in the Pathfinder calendar, typically takes place on the third Sabbath of September each year, where we celebrate what it means to be a Pathfinder. Every year, in advance of the day, resources are created and made available online to be used for this day. There is a theme for each year, and the day is mostly held outdoors, allowing for large gathering of young Pathfinders. The events of the day include singing, preaching, marching and drilling, and in some cases baptism. The latter requires careful planning as Bible studies would have to have taken place before the baptism. In my local Conference, Pathfinders who are taking part in the Pathfinder Bible Experience (PBE) are also encouraged to take part in instructive Bible studies leading up to baptism. As PBE is held at the beginning of the year, starting Bible studies at the same time allows many months of preparatory work to take place before the anticipated harvest later in the year.

Pathfinder Fair

Pathfinder Fair is another special event in the calendar, where Pathfinder clubs invite their families and spend a Sunday together. A Pathfinder Fair is generally organised by Conference Youth Director as a special day for the Pathfinder clubs. This day, club members come in full class A uniform from early in the morning up to late afternoon, exhibiting various demonstrations, marching and parading and partaking specialised skill events. Field uniform can also be worn during the time of activities. It is best organised during the sunny, warmer, summer months, to take advantage of longer daytime hours.

Each club takes part in traditional Pathfinder activities, range from knot tying, building items using lashings & natural materials, fire building, cooking, marching and lots more, that test the skills and teamwork of each club. This is great for the Pathfinders as they earn rewards based on their skills, teamwork and spirit.

Other Conferences have utilised the Pathfinder Fair as a fundraising event for the clubs that participate, when items sourced by the club are put up for sale from a stall, the proceeds going into the fundraising kit. All clubs attending are required to maintain a high standard of Pathfindering, showcase the array of skills during the skills demonstration, mix freely with other clubs to encourage fellowship and develop team spirit by undertaking tasks as a group. Parents and other church members are observers at this event, appreciating the work and skills of the Pathfinder staff and children, showing the interest of the church. Maybe, the most underestimated advantage of such an event is the opportunity of introducing and harnessing the Pathfinder ministry to the wider community through involvement of local community leaders.

The Pathfinder Fair may also be a time when individual or club awards are given in the spirit of striving for personal development rather than competition. When meticulously planned the fair can have a theme around which all the activities, events and displays are centred, creating a unified programme.

Pathfinder Rally

Pathfinder Rally is a time for clubs in a Conference to come together for fellowship and spiritual inspiration on a Sabbath once a year. The Conference Youth Director organises this event and usually seeks to hold it in a large public hall, church or auditorium. Some Conferences within a Union choose to hold a combined rally once in every few years, allowing for a larger gathering. Guests may include Division or Union Youth Directors. All Pathfinders and their leaders should be in full uniform and bring their club flag to the opening ceremony. The rally day offers an opportunity to harvest Pathfinders who have been undergoing Bible studies or even participating in the Pathfinder Bible experience (PBE) programme by conducting a baptism, which will inspire others to undertake future Bible studies. All in all, a rally day is an ideal time for parents, friends and church members to share the inspiration of Pathfinders.

Club Administration

One of the most important tasks for any Club Director is to make sure that the administrative tasks are fulfilled as *a stitch in time saves nine*. At the beginning of each Adventurer and Pathfinder curriculum year, an inventory of all the club members is collected, allocating each club member to the next achievement class following their successful class completion and investiture. This inventory of the club members offers the Director a unique panoramic view of club size and requirements. The club then performs an inventory of club assets such as camping equipment and first aid box. These are checked to make sure that they are in good condition and sufficient for the club size.

This list informs the Director on how many class workbooks to order for the club, how many club members to insure with the Conference and which Counsellors are allocated to teach each class. Little lambs class is usually parent-led, with parents helping their little lamb children to do their workbook at home or in Sabbath School. The other Adventurer classes will require Counsellors to teach, the number of Counsellors depending on the class size.

The Director, together with the club committee, makes sure that club rules and regulations are set and distributed to club members, parents and guardians. There is also a collection of significant data at the time of registration such as history of medical conditions and/or allergies. First aid and health and safety officers are given a mandate to establish safe practices for the club. The safe practices include, but are not limited to, developing guidance for the club to follow, to allow safeguarding practices to be in line with those of the church and making sure that a very healthy ratio of Counsellors to Adventurers or Pathfinders is always maintained at all times, with balance in gender mix. This is more important at group events such as sleepovers, local night camps, trips and camporees. The same principles of safe safeguarding practices are implemented when offering transportation to attend club activities, making sure that safeguarding policy is strictly followed at all times.

The local Club Director, liaising with the Local Conference Pathfinder Director, will order insignia, workbooks, and other materials that the club will use during the year. Some of the orders are to be done nearer the investiture time when honours and awards have been completed.

One last important detail in the club's administration is making sure that safeguarding and insurance policies are up to date and meet the requirements of the law. The club is advised not to start any club activities or meetings until all staff have gone through their mandatory safeguarding training and that insurance is in place for everyone in the club – children, staff and volunteers. These two – safeguarding and insurance policies and procedures – should be directly referred to the church board, so that the church is aware that these are in place.

Every club activity should have a risk assessment performed to ensure safety of everyone involved, from the Adventurers, Pathfinders and club leaders and staff. This is also more important if the activities involve travelling from your base. On such trips, a full medical record of each participant, full first aid provision, insurance – including medical cover, is required. This can be submitted to the local church board to get approval, prior to the trip.

Club administration checklist

1. **Year planner** – collate local club, Conference, and worldwide events into a yearly planner for the club

2. **Special Days** – collate and advertise the special days in the calendar such as club weekend campouts, hikes, nature walks/visits to national parks, aquarium or zoos, boat trips and Pathfinder banquet.

3. **Special events** – diarise the World Adventurer and Pathfinder Day, Rally Day, Pathfinder Fair, induction and investiture ceremonies.

4. **Conference events** – camporees, including international camporee

5. **Budget and Fundraising** – organise a team of passionate fundraisers to drive fundraising ventures

6. **Uniform** – order Class A Pathfinder uniforms and field uniforms for new inductees and take a uniform inventory/inspection for all the other Pathfinders

7. **Mandatory requirements** – Obtain club insurance and complete staff mandatory training courses, such as, safeguarding and keep the church family safe, Master Guide, Pathfinder Leadership Award (PLA) and Basic staff training

Club Uniform

Adventurer and Pathfinder clubs have designated uniforms, chosen by their respective Conferences, that identify their members and represent an ideal and standard of their calling. The uniform strengthens club spirit, appeals to would-be members and provides a real and visible presence in the community. The uniform is usually worn at club meetings, including but not limited to, induction and investiture services and at special events where the Adventurers and Pathfinders take part in as messengers, ushers, guards of honour, colour guards or first-aiders. Strict uniform standards are set by each Division of the SDA Church, based on the guidelines provided by the General Conference of the Church. So, every club must conform to these official standards. A full description of the class A uniform is provided in the appendix D, E and F, but here below, I have briefly outlined its composition. Field uniforms are mostly a local club matter, with the majority choosing their own club colour t/shirts and trousers/pants.

Adventurer Class A uniform

Adventurers' full class A uniform for girls is a navy-blue skirt, white blouse and white socks/tights. For boys, their corresponding uniform is navy blue pant, white shirt and black socks. Both genders will wear a burgundy scarf with an Adventurer slide that secures it and a navy-blue sash, worn from the right shoulder to the left hip. Adventurer stars, chips, awards, event patches, pins and other club related items may be displayed on the sash. The shoes are black with no added features. The emblems include the following: Adventurer patch (right sleeve), Adventurer world (left sleeve), club crescent (above Adventurer patch, right sleeve), Adventurer awards (on sash), camporee patches (on sash), and class pins (on shirt or blouse pocket).

Pathfinder Class A uniform

Pathfinders' full class A uniform for girls is a tan colour shirt or blouse which is long/short sleeved, with two pleated patch pockets with flaps on the chest and shoulder epaulets. The skirt is black in colour, has a pleated front, belt loops, and the hem should be at mid knee or below. Similarly, for boys, a tan coloured shirt which is long/short sleeved, with two pleated patch pockets with flaps on the chest and shoulder epaulets. The trousers are black in colour, with pleated front and belt loops. Both will wear green colour tie with club logo, scarf secured with Pathfinder Slide, black colour web belts with Pathfinder buckle, black shoes or boots with fully closed toe and heels, black socks, stockings or knee highs with no designs or patterns, black beret and a green fabric sash that is wide enough for up to 3 honours, and can have honours, camporee and fair patches and Pathfinder pins fixed. The sash is a personal club history of the Pathfinder, detailing his/her accomplishments and is worn over the right shoulder, under the neckerchief and preferably under the epaulet.

Meaning of the Pathfinder Club Emblem

All the parts (symbols and their colours) of the Pathfinder emblem have significant meaning, which should inform the Pathfinder. It is also useful for parents and guardians to grasp the meaning behind the chosen colours and symbols. Here I look at the full repertoire of the meanings.

Colours

Red represents blood/sacrifice which should constantly remind one of Christ's supreme sacrifice (John 3:16, Rom 12:1)

Gold represents excellence, the standard of measurement that we ascribe to as we prepare heavenly kingdom characters.

Blue represents loyalty to God in Heaven, Our parents (on earth) and our church, just like our true Master Guide, Jesus was.

White represents purity, as we ought to desire Christ's purity and His righteousness (Revelation 3:5)

Symbols

Triangle the three sides represent the unity and completeness of the Godhead - Father, Son, Holy Spirit. Similarly, these three sides represent the tripod of education pillars: mental (crafts and honours), physical (campouts) and spiritual (in and outreach) that form the cornerstone of the instruction.

Triangle is inverted to represent Jesus' self-sacrificial service, admonishing us to place the needs of others ahead of our own, as we emulate His example.

Shield represents protection that we get from the Word of God (Scripture, Ephesians 6:16) to fight the deceiver.

Sword represents the weapon (the Word of God/Bible) against the battle we are in (sin, great controversy)

Fundraising

Fundraising is an essential part of any club or non-profit organisation, helping them to gather the necessary resources and funding to support the various activities and initiatives. I explore some fundraising ideas that can be effective in raising the necessary funds for running the Adventurer and Pathfinder clubs.

One classic fundraising idea is organising a fundraising event. This can be a gala dinner, a charity auction, a fun run, or a talent show. Events like these provide a platform for like-minded people to come together, have fun, and donate to a common cause. Additionally, events often attract media attention and create a buzz in the community, which can lead to increased awareness and participation. To maximise the success of the fundraising event, advanced meticulous planning is required. This is where a dedicated fundraising team is invaluable, as the team focuses their energy on the events planned.

Another effective fundraising idea is selling products or merchandise. This can include items such as t-shirts, mugs, or other branded products. Many people are willing to support a cause by purchasing something tangible, and this can be a great way to raise funds while also increasing visibility for the cause.

Crowdfunding is a relatively new but effective fundraising strategy. There are many online platforms for crowdfunding such as JustGiving, Donorbox, GoFundMe, OneCause, Handbid, Bonfire, Fundly, Soapbox Engage, 99Pledges, Kickstarter and Mightycause which allow individuals to create online campaigns to gather donations from friends, family, and sometimes even from strangers. This approach is particularly effective for reaching a wide audience and tapping into the power of social media and online networks. Leveraging the power of technology and digital platforms can greatly enhance fundraising efforts. Online donations, mobile giving apps, and virtual events can all be effective ways to reach and engage potential donors.

Seeking sponsorships from local businesses or corporations can also be a successful fundraising strategy. Businesses might be willing to donate money or sponsor an event in exchange for public recognition, which can be a win-win for both parties.

Additionally, organising a raffle or a 50/50 draw can be a great way to raise funds. This is a simple and fun way for people to contribute, with the added incentive of potentially winning a prize.

There are numerous creative and effective fundraising ideas that can be utilized to raise the necessary funds for the clubs. By leveraging a combination of traditional and modern strategies, it is possible to engage a wide range of supporters and achieve fundraising goals. Ultimately, successful fundraising requires creativity, strategic planning, and effective communication to connect with potential donors and inspire them to contribute to the cause.

Innovative Practices

There has never been a better time for looking for innovative solutions to help deliver the Adventurer and Pathfinder ministries than during the time faced by the Covid-19 pandemic in 2020. The national lockdowns meant that Adventurer and Pathfinder clubs could no longer meet in the usual fashion. All face-to-face meetings were not allowed, creating difficulties in maintaining the ministries. However, several innovative solutions were pioneered using technology to deliver the programmes. Here, I take a look at some of the innovations that stood out.

Pathfinderskonekt

One example of an innovative idea that I came across was during the time I worked with Shamaine King, who was our Pathfinder Club Director during the lockdown years of the Covid-19 pandemic.

She knew straight away that with no face-to-face meetings allowed during the height of the pandemic, club meetings would have had to change dramatically, if the children were to continue fulfilling their curriculum requirements. She developed a way for the Adventurers and Pathfinders within our club to communicate and keep track of their work, by organising a dedicated online platform known as Pathfinderskonekt. This became a platform where parents and their children would get up-to-date information, curriculums/folders, all in one place. Classes had meeting rooms and could keep track of the work completed at any given time. Those who missed a class could easily catch up/return to a lesson. The platform made it easier for our club to interact in a safe space online. It suddenly grew to a point where two other clubs were invited to be part of the project, extending the benefits of online learning across the board. This big dream became a reality following extensive search for online website creation programmes.

Path-Fi Camporee "Unstoppable"

The first virtual/online camporee was organised and named The Unstoppable Path-Fi Camporee, held from 23 - 26 April 2020 during the Covid-19 pandemic. The Unstoppable Path-Fi Camporee was made open to any Pathfinder Club; however, each club was to be committed to taking part in each of the set challenges within the time allocated. The camporee was broadcast as a livestream on Facebook and YouTube, at set times.

Adventurer and Pathfinder E-clubs

The British Union Conference (BUC), through the great work of the Youth Ministries Leader, Pastor Dejan Stojkovic, launched a brand-new way to achieve Adventurer Awards and Pathfinder Honours during lockdown and times of social restrictions using Facebook live and Zoom video conferencing. The programmes were held on Saturday and Sunday afternoons for Adventurers and Pathfinders, respectively. A range of awards and honours including class requirements were taken online using Facebook live broadcast and Zoom video conferencing. The latter would only take limited numbers of participants whereas the former allowed for unlimited viewership. Hundreds of people joined from around the BUC and all over the world, becoming a part of this amazing online community at a time of great uncertainty. All the worksheets were completed at home under the guidance of the leader, these were marked and submitted as part of curriculum work. The greatest benefit was that these sessions are still available online on YouTube, which is handy for future use.

Pathfinder Allotment

Yes, you heard it correctly the first time around. One of the local clubs in West Yorkshire, England, Huddersfield, owned an allotment they used for gardening. The idea was that Pathfinders can come together, practice gardening and use the produce to raise funds by selling them to their church members. It worked so well, as the young people experienced a practical and outdoor lifestyle while learning important skills of team work and responsibility. This also provided an opportunity for the club itself to become partners with the local government, building strong bonds with the community.

Challenges

Pathfinder clubs are an essential part of many young people's lives, providing them with a sense of community, adventure, and personal growth. However, like any organization, Pathfinder clubs face their own set of challenges that can hinder their ability to effectively fulfil their mission. These challenges include financial constraints, recruitment and retention of members, and keeping up with the changing needs and interests of today's youth.

One of the biggest challenges facing Pathfinder clubs is financial constraints. Running a club requires funds for various activities, equipment, and resources. Many Pathfinder clubs operate on limited budgets, which can restrict the types of activities and experiences they are able to offer to their members. This can be particularly challenging for smaller clubs or those located in areas with limited financial resources. Finding creative ways to raise funds and secure sponsorships is essential in overcoming this hurdle.

Recruitment and retention of members is another significant challenge. In today's fast-paced world, young people have numerous options for extracurricular activities and may struggle to commit to long-term involvement in a single organisation. Pathfinder clubs must work hard to attract new members and create a welcoming and engaging environment to keep them coming back. This can be particularly difficult in areas where there is a lack of awareness about the club or where other extracurricular activities are more popular.

Furthermore, Pathfinder clubs also face the challenge of keeping up with the changing needs and interests of today's youth. The activities and experiences that were popular in the past may not necessarily resonate with today's young people. Clubs must constantly adapt and evolve their programming to ensure that they continue to appeal to their target audience. This may require investing in new equipment, training volunteers in new skills, or exploring new types of activities that align with the interests of today's youth.

In conclusion, Pathfinder clubs play an important role in the lives of young people, providing them with meaningful experiences and opportunities for personal growth. However, they face several challenges that can impact their ability to effectively fulfil their mission. By addressing issues such as financial constraints, recruitment and retention of members, and keeping up with the changing needs of today's youth, Pathfinder clubs can ensure that they remain relevant and impactful in the lives of the young people they serve.

The future of the Pathfinder club looks promising as it continues to evolve and adapt to the changing needs of today's youth. The Pathfinder club, which is a youth organization affiliated with the Seventh-day Adventist Church, aims to provide a supportive environment for young people to develop their spiritual, mental, and physical abilities. With a focus on community service, outdoor activities, and leadership development, the Pathfinder club has been a valuable resource for countless young people over the years.

As we look ahead to the future of the Pathfinder club, it is important to consider the ways in which the organization can continue to meet the needs of today's youth. This means staying relevant in a rapidly changing world and adapting to new technologies and social trends. The Pathfinder club must also continue to uphold its core values while embracing diversity and inclusivity.

One potential avenue for the future of the Pathfinder club is the integration of technology into its programming. As young people become increasingly reliant on digital devices and online communication, the Pathfinder club can leverage technology to engage and educate its members. This could involve the development of online resources, virtual meetings and events, and the use of social media to connect with young people.

Another important aspect of the future of the Pathfinder club is its commitment to diversity and inclusivity. As our society becomes more diverse, it is critical that the Pathfinder club reflects and celebrates this diversity. This means creating programming and resources that are accessible and welcoming to young people from all backgrounds. It also means actively addressing issues of equality and justice within the organization and in the wider community.

In addition to these considerations, the future of the Pathfinder club will also depend on its ability to maintain strong leadership and mentorship. The club has always been driven by dedicated adult leaders who provide guidance, support, and encouragement to its members. As the club continues to grow and evolve, it will be essential to recruit and develop new leaders who can effectively mentor and inspire the next generation of Pathfinders.

Overall, the future of the Pathfinder club looks bright as it continues to adapt to the needs of today's youth. By embracing technology, diversity, and strong leadership, the club can continue to provide a valuable and enriching experience for young people for many years to come.

The future of the Pathfinder club is bright and promising. As we continue to navigate through the ever-changing landscape of youth development and education, the Pathfinder club remains a vital and relevant organization that plays a crucial role in shaping the lives of young people.

In the coming years, we can envision the Pathfinder club evolving and adapting to meet the needs and interests of today's youth. We foresee the incorporation of modern technology and innovative teaching methods to make the club even more engaging and impactful. By embracing new trends and advancements, the Pathfinder club can continue to capture the attention and enthusiasm of young members, while also preparing them for the challenges and opportunities of the 21st century.

Furthermore, we anticipate a greater emphasis on global citizenship and environmental stewardship within the Pathfinder club. As the world becomes more interconnected and environmentally conscious, it is essential for young people to develop a strong sense of social responsibility and an understanding of the natural world. Through meaningful service projects, outdoor adventures, and education on global issues, the Pathfinder club can instil in its members a deep appreciation for the planet and a desire to make a positive impact in their communities and beyond.

In addition, we envision the continued growth and expansion of the Pathfinder club worldwide. As more communities recognize the value and impact of the organization, we expect to see an increase in the number of clubs and members across different countries and cultures. This global reach will not only enrich the experiences of Pathfinder members, but also promote cross-cultural understanding and unity among young people from diverse backgrounds.

Ultimately, the future of the Pathfinder club is one of endless possibilities. With a dedicated and passionate leadership team and a supportive network of parents and volunteers, the club is well-positioned to thrive and continue making a difference in the lives of young people. By staying true to its core values of leadership, service, and personal development, the Pathfinder club can look forward to a future filled with opportunities to inspire and empower the next generation of leaders and change-makers.

The future

I recall a ubiquitous slogan for a UK telecommunications company titled "The future's bright, the future's Orange". The catchy slogan lasted only 14 years before the slogan and the company were consigned to history. However, our young people can put all their trust in Jesus Christ and be assured of a bright future, one promised by Jesus.

The future is bright with Jesus on our side. We can embrace the future with all the technological developments while remaining true to the values of Adventurer and Pathfinder ministry. For example, when the Covid-19 pandemic in 2020 caused countries to go into lockdown, the Adventure and Pathfinder ministries relied on the digital platforms for videoconferencing to continue to meet the needs of the young people, holding virtual club meetings, virtual Bible Experience testing and virtual investiture services, camporees and World Adventurer and Pathfinder Days.

One of the areas where the Adventurer and Pathfinder ministries would do well is to embrace all the digital platforms to meet young people on the digital platforms where they spend most of their time. For example, our young people could use their social media presence to evangelise to the world.

Another strong area to venture into is the collaboration with society through national events such as independence celebrations, national ceremonies, using our unique skills in drumming, drilling and marching to be at the centre of the celebrations.

About the author

Born Mandela Thyoka in Malawi, Dr Mandela Thyoka grew up in Zimbabwe in his early formative years before returning to his native Malawi. He read Medicine at University of St Andrew's, Fife, Scotland and University College London. He has been a Church Elder, Primary School Governor, Pathfinder Director and Sponsor. Dr Thyoka writes this book as a parent, club Counsellor and Director.

For Dr Mandela Thyoka, Pathfindering has always been more about a way of life, leading children and young people to Jesus Christ. Sharing treasured experiences from his early years as an Adventurer and a Pathfinder to his leadership roles in both ministries, this book seeks to pivot these ministries on helping parents and their children develop a lasting relationship with Jesus Christ. This is all that matters.

In Adventurers and Pathfinders: Living for Jesus, he shares the blueprint of successful Pathfindering, from developing an early interest in children about knowing Jesus to the point where they develop a deeper and lasting saving relationship with Jesus. Everything offered within both clubs is all about Jesus, from the curriculum that includes activities, awards and honours, to everything else. In this book, Christian author Mandela Thyoka shares a comprehensive exploration of the perfect way parents should think about Pathfindering and teaches them how to help their children make better sense of one of life's most important decision - living for Jesus.

Through the wholesome experiences in the Adventure and Pathfinder clubs, children can positively impact their friends at church, school, and the wider community, through Kingdom living. Their citizenry of this world is enhanced while remaining true to the higher calling for the heavenly citizenry. Progressing through all the curricula stages, children become transformed, and their path illuminated to reach their full potential and live victoriously for Jesus.

Acknowledgement

I thank my awesome wife, Tumpale, for being my pillar of strength especially during the time I spent writing this book. She was there for our children, Tawonga, Vitumbiko and Tuwemi, who are today's Adventurers and Pathfinders, when I spent hours immersed in writing. Thank you so much.

Secondly, I thank my late parents, mum and dad. Together, they made sure they gave me the opportunity to embrace the spirit of Adventurer and Pathfinder clubs, from my early days in Malawi and Zimbabwe. I wholeheartedly dedicate this book to the memory of my late parents.

Lastly, this book would not have been possible without God's grace and power. In Jesus Christ, the Supreme Pathfinder, I found the strength to lead young people to Him.

Appendix A. Adventurers and Pathfinders Club activities

Club induction service – lighting up class candles

Club investiture service – candidate receiving an award

North England Conference Drill and Drum Team

Hiking, Bolton Abbey Estate, North Yorkshire, UK

Conference Rally Day parade, Hull City, UK

Doncaster Doves Adventurer Bible Experience team

South England Conference Camporee, Hertfordshire, UK

International camporee, Oshkosh, Wisconsin, USA

Appendix B. Adventurer Stars, Chips, and Awards

Adventurers learn best by exploring their world and being creative. The patches they earn on completion are called stars for the Little Lambs, chips for Early Birds and awards for Busy Bees through to Helping Hands. There are more than **150** Adventurer Stars, Chips, and Awards available for completion. The full list is as below.

Little Lamb Stars (21)
ABC's
Bible Friends
Bodies of Water
Colours
Community Helper
Finger Play
Healthy Food
Healthy Me
Insects
Little Boy Jesus
Music
My Friend Jesus
Numbers
Sharing
Special Helper
Stars
Trains and Trucks
Trikes & Bikes
Weather
Wooly Lamb
Zoo Animals

Early Bird Chips (27)
Alphabet Fun
Animal Homes

Animals
Beaver
Beginning Biking
Beginning Swimming
Bible Friends (EB)
Birds
Crayons and Markers
Fire Safety
Gadgets And Sand
God's World
Helping at Home
Jesus' Special Helper
Jesus' Star
Jigsaw Puzzle
Know Your Body
Left And Right
Manners Fun
My Community Friends
Pets
Playing With Friends
Scavenger Hunt
Shapes And Sizes
Sponge Art
Stamping Fun
Toys

Busy Bee Awards (17)
Artist
Bible I
Butterfly
Buttons
Fish
Flowers
Friend of Animals
Guide

Health Specialist
Home Helper
Music Maker
Potato
Reading I
Safety Specialist
Sand Art
Spotter
Swimmer I

Sunbeam Awards (22)
Acts of Kindness
BakingSunbeam
Camper
Collector
Cooking Fun
Courtesy
Feathered Friends
Fitness Fun
Friend of Jesus
Friend of Nature
Gardener
Glue Right
Handicraft
Ladybugs
Missionaries
Reading II
Road Safety
Seasons
Seeds
Skier
Trees
Whales

Builder Awards (28)
Astronomer
Bead Craft
Build & Fly
Building Blocks
Cyclist
Disciples
Early Adventist Pioneer
Family Helper
First Aid Helper
Gymnast
Hand Shadows
Homecraft
Honey
Lizards
Magnet Fun
Magnet Fun II
Media Critic
Olympics
Postcards
Prayer
Reading III
Saving Animals
Sewing Fun
Swimmer II
Temperance
Tin Can Fun
Troubadour
Wise Steward

Helping Hand Awards (28)
Basket Maker
Bible II
Bible Royalty
Caring Friend

Carpenter
Technology (formerly Computer Skills)
Country Fun
Environmentalist
Fruits of the Spirit
Geologist
Habitat
Honey Bee
Hygiene
My Church
My Picture Book
Outdoor Explorer
Pearly Gates
Prayer Warrior
Rainbow Promise
Reading IV
Reporter
Safe Water
Sign Language
Skater
Stamp Art
Steps to Jesus
Tabernacle
Weather

Multi-Level Awards (11)
Bible Storytelling
Bread of Life
Cooperation
Delightful Sabbath
Dogs
Good Samaritan
Listening
Parables of Jesus
Photo Fun

Stay Safe
Universe

Special Award Patches (3)
Adventurer's Evangelism Patch
Adventurer's Excellence in Reading Patch
Adventurer Bible Experience (ABE) pin

Appendix C. Pathfinder Honours

Similarly, Pathfinders, like Adventurers, have fun ways of learning new skills in the following categories: Arts & Crafts, Health & Science, Household Arts, Nature, Outdoor Industries, Recreation, Vocational and Spiritual Growth, Outreach and Heritage. There are more than **500** Pathfinder honours available for completion, as listed below.

Arts & Crafts (104)
Aboriginal Lore
African Lore
Airplane Modeling
Basketry
Block Printing
Braiding
Currency – Advanced
Braiding – Advanced
Bread Dough
Bridges
Cake Decorating
Digital Photography
Candle Making
Card Making
Ceramics
Copper Enameling
Copper Enameling – Advanced
Counted Cross Stitch
Crocheting
Crocheting – Advanced
Currency
Drawing
Drawing – Advanced
Duct Tape
Découpage
Felt Craft

Flower Arrangement
Genealogy
Genealogy - Advanced
Gift Wrapping
Glass Craft
Glass Etching
Glass Painting
Guitar
Guitar - Advanced
Hot Air Balloons
Kanzashi
Knitting
Knitting - Advanced
Lapidary
Leather Craft
Leather Craft - Advanced
LEGO® Design
Lettering & Poster Making
Lighthouses
Lighthouses - Advanced
Macramé
Māori Lore
Metal Craft
Model Boats
Model Cars
Model Railroad
Model Rocketry
Model Rocketry
Mosaic Tile
Music
Music - Advanced
Native American Lore
Native American Lore - Advanced
Native Brush Construction
Needle Craft
Origami

Painting
Painting - Advanced
Paper Maché
Paper Quilling
Paper Quilling - Advanced
Photography
Pin Trading
Pin Trading – Advanced
Pinewood Derby
Pinewood Derby - Advanced
Plaster Craft
Plastic Canvas
Plastic Canvas - Advanced
Plastics
Poetry and Songwriting
Postcards
Postcards - Advanced
Pottery
Scrapbooking
Scrapbooking - Advanced
Sculpturing
Silk Screen Printing
Silk Screen Printing - Advanced
Soap Craft
Soap Craft - Advanced
Spinning Yarn
Stamps
Stamps - Advanced
Street Art
String Art
Textile Painting
Thatching
Tie-Dye
Tole Painting
Upholstery
Weaving

Whistles
Whistles - Advanced
Wood Carving
Wood Handicraft
Toy Boat Regatta
Toy Boat Regatta – Advanced

Health & Science (19)
Basic Rescue
Biosafety
Blood and the Body's Defenses
Bones, Muscles, and Movement
Brain and Behaviour
Chemistry
CPR
Digestion
First Aid - Advanced
First Aid, Basic
First Aid, Standard
Health and Healing
Heart and Circulation
Heredity
Home Nursing
Optics
Physics
Red Alert
Viruses

Household Arts (20)
Baking
Basic Sewing
Cooking
Cooking - Advanced
Cultural Food Preparation

Dressmaking
Dressmaking - Advanced
Food - Canning
Food - Drying
Food - Freezing
Household Budgeting
Housekeeping
Laundering
Mat Making
Nutrition
Nutrition - Advanced
Pizza Maker
Quilting
Tailoring
Tapa Cloth

Nature (115)
Alternative Fuels
Alternative Fuels - Advanced
Amphibians
Amphibians - Advanced
Animal Camouflage
Animal Camouflage - Advanced
Animal Tracking
Animal Tracking - Advanced
Antelopes
Antelopes - Advanced
Bats
Bats - Advanced
Bird Pets
Birds
Birds - Advanced
Bogs & Fens
Bogs & Fens - Advanced
Bubbles

Cacti
Cacti - Advanced
Cats
Cats - Advanced
Cetaceans
Climate Science
Climate Science - Advanced
Coral Reefs
Coral Reefs - Advanced
Dinosaurs
Dog Care and Training
Dogs
Dunes
Dunes - Advanced
Ecology
Ecology - Advanced
Edible Wild Plants
Endangered Species
Environmental Conservation
Eucalypts
Ferns
Fishes
Flowers
Flowers - Advanced
Fossils
Fungi
Geology
Geology - Advanced
Grasses
Herbs
House Plants
Insects
Insects - Advanced
Lichens, Liverworts & Mosses
Livestock
Mammals

Mammals - Advanced
Maple Sugar
Maple Sugar –
Marine Algae
Marine Invertebrates
Marine Mammals
Marsupials
Meteorites
Microscopic Life
Midnight Sun
Moths & Butterflies
Mountains
Odonates
Odonates - Advanced
Orchids
Palm Trees
Parrots and Cockatoos
Poultry
Rainforests
Raptors
Raptors - Advanced
Recycling
Renewable Energy
Reptiles
Reptiles - Advanced
Rivers and Streams
Rivers and Streams - Advanced
Rocks & Minerals
Rocks & Minerals - Advanced
Sand
Seeds
Seeds - Advanced
Sharks
Shells
Shells - Advanced
Shrubs

Small Mammal Pets
Soils
Spiders
Stars
Stars - Advanced
Taiga
Taiga - Advanced
Temperate Deciduous Forests
Trees
Trees - Advanced
Water Science
Water Science - Advanced
Waterfalls
Wattles
Weather
Weather - Advanced
Worms
Worms - Advanced
Migration
Oceans
Predatory Plants
Grasslands
Temperate Grasslands
Temperate Grasslands - Advanced

Outdoor Industries (17)
Agriculture
Beekeeping
Cattle Husbandry
Dairying
Flower Culture
Fruit Growing
Gardening
Goat Husbandry
Horse Husbandry

Island Fishing
Pigeon Raising
Poultry Raising
Sheep Husbandry
Small Fruit Growing
Subsistence Farming
Hydroponics and Aquaponics
Hydroponics and Aquaponics - Advanced

Recreation (109)
Abseiling
Abseiling - Advanced
Abseiling - Instructor
Adapted Sports
Archery
Archery - Advanced
Backpacking
Backpacking - Advanced
Basic Water Safety
Basketball
Camp Craft
Camp Safety
Camp Safety - Advanced
Camping Skills I
Camping Skills II
Camping Skills III
Camping Skills IV
Canoe Building
Canoeing
Canoeing - Advanced
Caving
Caving - Advanced
Cold Weather Survival
Cycling
Cycling - Advanced

Drilling & Marching
Drilling & Marching - Advanced
Drumming & Percussion
Drumming & Percussion - Advanced
Dutch Oven Cooking
Fire Building & Camp Cookery
Flag Football
Geocaching
Geocaching - Advanced
Geological Geocaching
Geological Geocaching - Advanced
Gold Prospecting
Golf
Hiking
Horsemanship
Horsemanship - Advanced
Juggling
Kayaking
Kites
Knot Tying
Lashing
Lashing - Advanced
Letterboxing
Letterboxing - Advanced
Lifesaving
Lifesaving - Advanced
Mountain Biking
Navigation
Orienteering
Outdoor Leadership
Outdoor Leadership - Advanced
Physical Fitness
Pickleball
Pioneering
Power Boating
Rock Climbing

Rock Climbing - Advanced
Rowing
SailingRec
Scuba Diving
Scuba Diving - Advanced
Skateboarding
Skiing - Cross Country
Skiing Downhill
Skin Diving
Slow-Pitch Softball
Snowshoeing
Snowshoeing - Advanced
Soccer
Springboard Diving
Swimming
Swimming - Advanced
Swimming - Beginner
Swimming - Beginner - Advanced
Swimming - Intermediate
Tennis
Tents
Track & Field
Travel
Travel - Advanced
Tree Climbing
Triathlon
Triathlon - Advanced
Tumbling & Balancing
Tumbling & Balancing - Advanced
Ultimate Disc
Ultimate Disc - Advanced
Unicycling
Volleyball
Wakeboarding
Water Safety Instructor
Water Safety Instructor - Advanced

Water Skiing
Water Skiing - Advanced
Wilderness Leadership
Wilderness Leadership - Advanced
Wilderness Living
Wind Surfing
Winter Camping
Community Water Safety - Advanced
National Parks and Heritage Sites
National Parks and Heritage Sites - Advanced
Community Water Safety
Disc Golf

Spiritual Growth, Outreach and Heritage (73)
Adventist Pioneer Heritage
Adventurer for Christ
Adventurer for Christ - Advanced
African American Adventist Heritage in the NAD
African American Adventist Heritage in the NAD - Advanced
Alive Bible
Bible Marking
Bible Marking - Advanced
Biblical Archaeology
Braille
Bully Prevention I
Bully Prevention II
Child Care
Christian Art of Preaching
Christian Art of Preaching - Advanced
Christian Citizenship
Christian Drama
Christian Grooming & Manners
Christian Storytelling
Christian Team Building

Christian Visitation
Community Improvement
Creationism
Creationism - Advanced
Crisis Intervention
Cultural Diversity Appreciation
Disaster Ministries
Disciples and Apostles
Family Life
Feeding Ministries
Flags
Flags - Advanced
Foreign Mission Trips
God's Messenger
Hymns
Identifying Community Needs
Judges of Israel
Junior Youth Leadership
Kings of Israel
Literature Evangelism
Media Broadcast Ministry
Missionary Life
Parade Floats
Parade Floats - Advanced
Patriarchs of the Bible
Peace Maker
Peace Maker - Advanced
Personal Evangelism
Praise and Worship
Prayer
Prayer - Advanced
Preach It
Preach It - Advanced
Prophets & Prophecy
Prophets & Prophecy - Advanced
Puppetry

Puppetry - Advanced
Refugee Assistance
Rural Development
Sanctuary
Sanctuary - Advanced
Serving Communities
Sign Language
Sign Language - Advanced
Small Group Bible Study
Small Group Bible Study - Advanced
Stewardship
Tutoring
Sabbath Appreciation
Three Angels' Messages
Women in Adventist History

Vocational (61)
Accounting
Artificial Intelligence
Automobile Mechanics
Automobile Mechanics - Advanced
Aviators
Barbering and Hairstyling
Bible Evangelism
Blacksmithing
Bookbinding
Bookkeeping
Business
Carpentry
Christian Sales Principles
Communications
Communications - Advanced
Computers
Computers - Advanced
Electricity

Engineering
Fire Safety
Forestry
Forestry - Advanced
House Painting, Exterior
House Painting, Interior
Internet
Internet - Advanced
Journalism
Masonry
Mobile Technology
Paperhanging
Plumbing
Printing
Radio
Radio - Advanced
Radio Electronics
Robotics
Robotics - Advanced
Shoe Repair
Shorthand
Small Engines
Soap Making
Soap Making - Advanced
Social Media
Teaching
Tile Laying
Typewriting
Video
Video - Advanced
Visual Media Critique
Welding
Woodworking
Word Processing
Computers and Mobile Devices
Computers and Mobile Devices - Advanced

Dams & Hydroelectricity
Pewter Casting
Land Surveying
Drones
Signs, Signals and Symbols
Welding
Video

Arts & Crafts (25)
Aboriginal Lore
African Lore
Airplane Modeling
Basketry
Block Printing
Braiding
Currency – Advanced
Braiding – Advanced
Bread Dough
Bridges
Cake Decorating
Digital Photography
Candle Making
Card Making
Ceramics
Copper Enameling
Copper Enameling – Advanced
Counted Cross Stitch
Crocheting
Crocheting – Advanced
Currency
Drawing
Drawing – Advanced
Duct Tape
Découpage

Appendix D. Pathfinder Uniform and Insignia

The Pathfinder uniform and correctly placed insignia are worn as in the diagram below. Here is a 10-point guidance of the insignia.

1. *Pathfinder Honour Sash.* The sash is worn over the right shoulder, under the scarf and under the left arm. Notice that the sash forms a diagonal from right shoulder at the top to the bottom left side of the body at its lower point and the upper part of the sash covers the right pocket. The sash is wide enough allowing honours to be placed on its front and tokens for Camporees, Expeditions, Fairs and Campouts placed on the back of the sash. When the sash is full of tokens, the sash can be updated, or a new sash is obtained.

2. *Pathfinder Scarf.* The scarf is worn around the neck, over the sash and held in place with the Pathfinder woggle. The scarf has the world emblem on the back peak. The Pathfinder woggle is a gold cylinder with the Pathfinder world emblem on it and is used to hold the scarf in place.

3. *Beret.* The beret is worn over the head but can also be placed, folded, over the left shoulder.

4. *Class Insignia.* Pathfinder receives a badge for each class successfully invested and this badge is worn on the left pocket as a pocket strip and a class chevron is worn on the left sleeve.

5. *Pathfinder tie.* The tie is worn in the usual fashion and can be tucked in between the third and fourth front button of the Pathfinder shirt.

6. *Club Name Strip.* The right sleeve of the pathfinder short is a place where club name strip, staff name strip (only for staff) and Pathfinder emblem are located. The topmost of these, the club name strip is worn above the staff name strip and Pathfinder emblem on the right sleeve.

7. *Staff Name Strip.* The district director, club director, deputy director, chaplain, instructor, counsellor and junior counsellor wear a name strip, designating their position, above the Pathfinder emblem on the right sleeve and below the club name strip.

8. *Pathfinder Emblem.* The 7.5 cm emblem is triangular and is the lowest emblem to be worn on the right sleeve. Pathfinders will wear their Pathfinder emblem 1.5cm directly below the club name, as they do not wear the staff name strip.

9. *Conference Patch.* The conference patch is 6.5m tall and is worn over the left sleeve, 1.5cm above the world emblem.
10. *Pathfinder World Emblem.* This oval symbol, which contains the Pathfinder emblem, representing the worldwide organisation of Pathfinder clubs of the Seventh-day Adventist Church, is worn on the left sleeve, 1.5cm below the Conference patch.

The following are not shown in the diagram.

11. *Class Chevron* (not labelled but can be seen on the left sleeve diagram shown). This coloured sleeve strip is a part of the class insignia representing each class completed and should be worn on the left sleeve, 1.5cm below the Pathfinder World Emblem.
12. *Captain and Scribe Badges* (not shown). These are worn by captains and scribes on the sash or positioned above the right pocket (if sash is removed).
13. *Chaplain Badge* (not shown). This is worn by a club chaplain on the sash or positioned above the right pocket (if sash is removed).
14. *Belt Buckle with Pathfinder Emblem* (not shown). The Pathfinder triangular emblem is engraved on the belt buckle.
15. *Pathfinder Award of Excellence.* The left pocket may have advanced class bars immediately above the class insignia, and the Pathfinder Award of Excellence, which is awarded at a conference event, is worn above these.

Appendix E. Adventurer Class A Uniform Inspection

Name of Club
_____

Adventurer Inspection	Points
Bible in left hand	
Scarf, Sky Blue / Green with logo new adventurer burgundy scarf	
Adventurer woggle	
Sash, Navy Blue – Awards on the front/ events on the back	
Shirt / Blouse: White long sleeves	
Left Sleeve: Adventurer world	
Right Sleeve: Club name	
Trousers/Skirt: Navy blue	
Girls: White socks or tights (whether short or long, all wearing the same)	
Black shoes	
Adventurer Pledge and Law	
	Total:
Club Director Signature	
Inspector's signature and printed name Please print name here	

Each item is 1 point

Appendix F. Pathfinder Class A Uniform Inspection

Name of Club
_____

Pathfinder Inspection	Points
Bible in left hand	
Beret, Black with 2" logo	
Scarf, Pathfinder with logo	
Pathfinder woggle	
Sash, green – Honours on the front & events on the back	
4" logo at bottom of sash	
FAD Shirt	
Pathfinder tie with logo	
Left Sleeve: Conference Patch, Pathfinder world Patch	
Class chevron	
Right Sleeve: Club name, 3" logo	
Shirt front, good conduct, class tab and pins	
Male: trousers plain black	
Male: Pathfinder buckle	
Female: Regulation Pathfinder skirt	
Female: Pathfinder buckle	
Plain black tights; black shoes	
Pathfinder Pledge and Law	
	Total:
Club Director Signature	
Inspector's signature and printed name Please print name here	

Each item is 1 point

References

General Conference Corporation of Seventh-day Adventist Youth Ministries Department. *Teacher's Resource Manual How to Teach the Adventurer Classes*. General Conference of Seventh-day Adventists, 2004.

General Conference Corporation of Seventh-day Adventist Youth Ministries Department. *Pathfinder Administrative Manual*. General Conference of Seventh-day Adventists, 2004.

John Hancock. *The Pathfinder Story*. Advent Source, 2004.

North American Division Youth Ministries Department. *Investiture Achievement Director's Guide*. AdventSource, 2014.

North American Division Youth Ministries Department. *Master Guide Club Manual*. AdventSource, 2022.

North American Division Youth Ministries Department. *Teen Leadership Training Directors Guide*. AdventSource, 2014.

North American Division Youth Ministries Department. *The Pathfinder Bible Experience Application Guide*. AdventSource, 2023-2024.

www.ingramcontent.com/pod-product-compliance
Lightning Source LLC
Chambersburg PA
CBHW050236120526
44590CB00016B/2116